The Demolition
of Democracy

The Demolition of Democracy

Has America Lost Its Soul

Tyranny
Racism
Unhinged
Misogynistic
Prejudice

∞

Ted Bagley

Matchstick Literary
1-888-306-8885
www.matchliterary.com
orders@matchliterary.com

Contents

PREFACE

The writing of this book was motivated by what I view as a disappearing moralistic value gene in the body and soul of America with new realities developing every day under the new Trump administration. Donald J. Trump was inaugurated on January 20, 2017, which started a decline in morality, respect, and dignity not seen in this country since the horrors of slavery. For the first time in my life, I feel that there is a racist thumb on the scale of justice by this current Trump administration.

You can see his failure to label the activities of white supremacists as such, his embrace of alt-right and other racist groups as "good people," his vicious attacks on Senator John McCain even after his death, and his misuse of the presidential powers in declaring a national emergency just to get a wall that will do very little to secure our borders. Think about it. President Trump simply wants a symbol to point to long after he is gone, something that will have his stamp on it. He would, if allowed, place a golden calf at each end of the wall as a symbol for those of his cult to worship him and boast of his victory of evil over good.

I have had to make continued changes to my script because of the organized chaos of this administration. My father would always tell me that there was nothing that I couldn't do if I put my mind and body to work. He would say, "Dream the impossible dream and stretch your horizons." I have taken him at his word. I have been fairly successful in my career, rising to vice president of a major corporation. I have written four books and have traveled the world, but never have I encountered an environment as toxic as the current one. Never have I experienced the hatred and bias that is ripping at the soul of a nation as the current environment does.

President Trump and his band of misfits have developed a culture of impunity in the White House, which will leave stains on this country for years to come. They operate as if they are above the law, and many are beginning to believe that they are. One example is the Trump administration's failure to hold Saudi Arabia responsible for the October 2018 killing of US-based journalist Jamal Khashoggi. No one on the Republican side of the aisle or the Congress, for that matter, took them to task for it. It seems that this administration is more concerned with current and future business deals and their political careers than they are about human rights violations or taking on a president who is so obviously unfit to serve as the most powerful figure in the world.

Many are saying that this is our new reality, but I don't buy into that. It will be our new reality if we allow it to be. What can we do, you ask, to combat this Hitler-like leader? Vote, run for office, educate yourself, attend city council meetings, and let your voice be heard. Dead men and women walking will never be able to affect change. It takes having courage of candor, speaking truth to power, and stepping out on faith to change the hearts and souls of a nation.

ACKNOWLEDGMENTS

IN ANY WORK of this nature, there are those who play a very supportive role in bringing the project to, hopefully, a successful conclusion. In attempting to write such a book, it's vitally necessary to get the perspectives of different facets of the community to validate opinions and even factual information.

One such resource is a friend and confidant who was significantly helpful in sharing the international perspective. As a result of being a native of the eastern European country located in eastern Europe across the Adriatic Sea from Italy, his perspective added greatly to the international view of this administration. He has opinions and knowledge of our politics well beyond his years. It was of vital importance that I have the perspective of those who view us from afar and who have lived the international experience.

No work would be complete without another set of eyes to edit the project. This person was none other than Monica Walker of Atlanta, Georgia. Monica, an educator and family member, was chosen for this role because of her patience, attention to detail, and excellent verbal and analytical skills. I know, without a doubt, that if there are passages in this work that Monica has a strong opinion about from a negative perspective, I will hear about it in no uncertain terms. Her tireless efforts in editing this work while carrying on her daily classroom schedule were simply phenomenal. Finally, in the Acknowledgment, please add this statement. Thanks to my wife Debra for taking a final look and catching a few changes prior to final edit. She has an eye for the detail.

I also dedicate this book to all who chose to vote for this self-proclaimed "superhero" Donald J. Trump. I do see some relative similarities between this new administration and the likes of other superheroes such as Spiderman, Superman, and Batman. His administration may not be able to fly or subdue villains, but they are good at spinning a web of lies and deceit. He is more knowledgeable than his generals, smarter than the Joint Chiefs, and is a physical specimen in his words. Now the similarities to superheroes are beginning to come into focus, especially the characteristic of spinning a web. You would have to admit that this president, in his first term in office, has appointed "villain-like" individuals to key positions; and as a result, several are serving time for lying to Congress or involving themselves in actions that were detrimental to the sovereignty of the United States. See you between the pages.

CHAPTER 1

The Dissecting of a Democracy

The ship of Democracy, which has weathered all storms, may sink through the mutiny of those aboard.

—Grover Cleveland

I T IS IMPORTANT to define a democracy before we can surmise that it is at risk of being dissected or destroyed. A democracy is a government in which the supreme power is *vested* in the people and exercised by them directly or indirectly through a system of representation usually involving periodically held free *elections*; the political direction and control exercised over the actions of the members, citizens, or inhabitants of communities, societies, and states; direction of the affairs of a state, community, etc.; political administration. *Government is necessary to the existence of civilized society.*

In the title, it speaks of the destruction of our form of government and a possible new reality. The signals that we should all be concerned are rooted in behaviors such as suppressing voters, gerrymandering (changing the size of districts), lying without remorse, destroying the prior administration's accomplishments, not taking the advice of seasoned generals concerning international policy, taking kids away from parents in the name of good border security, shutting down the government because of a failed attempt to get US taxpayers to pay for a wall that he said would be paid for by the Mexican government, and claiming ultimate victory over the Islamic State (ISIS) without substantiating facts. Now you get the picture.

Are we operating as part of a democracy or under this administration? Are we a part of a kleptocracy, which is a government with corrupt leaders who use their power to exploit the people and natural resources of their own territory in order to extend their personal wealth and political powers? The Republican Party, which had a Regan flair, is now the party of Trump, which does not fare well for the party.

Trump, with his celebrity and incredulity toward those who oppose him, has created a stage for himself that could change the presidency for decades to come. We have gone from a charismatic, negotiating, competent, caring president in President Obama to one who seems to be immoral, misogynistic, verbally incompetent, and unworthy in Trump. His bullying style seems just what the political right wanted, it seems.

No matter how insane this president acts, the Republican majority and his base fail and refuse to hold this political misfit in check. He attacks those who do not look like him or share his views, whoever they are. He thrives off name-calling, labeling, fake-news rants, tweets, golf, and a diet of cheeseburgers.

Is President Trump a racist? I believe with certainty that this man is a racist and would turn on his own mother if she disagrees with him. You judge a man not by what he says but by what he does and the company he keeps. He attacks black football players, immigrants, women, Latinos; refused to give proper assistance to Puerto Rico after the hurricane; and called countries with predominantly black and brown people "shithole countries." Now you decide whether he is racist or not.

The country is in desperate need of leadership both domestically and internationally but, for sure, not Trump's style of leadership. The attitudes and behaviors of certain segments of the country are embarrassing to say the least. This new reality of a country is not the one that I have grown to love and respect over the years. Race and gender aside, the soul of this country, along with a brand that has withstood the test of time, is under vicious attack from this self-deprecating, disrespecting individual. I can say without hesitation, there has never been one like him, and thank God for that.

As of May 2018, there have been twenty-two school shootings in the past year. Many of these atrocities are enabled by the lack of action on gun control by the president and the United States Congress. This Congress and this president have chosen to believe that the NRA (National Rifle Association) is too powerful of a lobby to challenge. They chose not to legislate gun control but instead point the blame of the horrific killings of our young minds on mental illness on the part of the perpetrator. *Mental illness* refers to a wide range of mental health conditions and disorders that affect your mood, thinking, and behavior. It most definitely is an illness, but one of hate and vindictiveness.

Every year, approximately 42.5 million American adults (or 18.2 percent of the total adult population in the United States) suffer from some form of mental illness, causing conditions such as depression, bipolar disorder, or schizophrenia. Nice try, but mass shootings represent a small percentage of all gun violence, and mental illness is not a factor in most violent acts. According to one epidemiological estimate, eliminating the effects of mental illness would only reduce all violence by 4 percent.

Again, nice try, GOP, Trump, and the NRA. Your pitch primarily to your base as well as those whom you have mentally manipulated may have a significant impact on what they think or believe but not on those of us who were not mesmerized by your rhetoric. We know gun violence is a public health problem because more than thirty thousand people a year are dying from it. It is the third leading cause of death for American children. That in itself should be enough to get the lawmakers motivated to act. Anecdotally speaking, Americans are more likely than people in similar nations to be shot in church, in school, at a concert, in movie houses, or in a town hall. The malignancy of failure to enact a law dealing with these weapons of mass destruction has created this new reality that has thrust our schools and our children in a cycle of copycat killings unseen in modern history.

This cowardly administration and their Fox News / NRA advocates have changed what was a dream for a better world into a seemingly never-ending nightmare. This current administration, because of their controlling the three branches of government (executive, legislative, and judicial), continues to cater to the gun lobbyist at the expense of our young minds. Paul Ryan, *who was* Speaker of the House at the writing of this book, and Mitch McConnell, Senate majority leader, are proving to be empty shirts, unable to think for themselves and afraid of jeopardizing their political careers because of the vindictive nature of this president.

I am writing this book with relentlessness and indefatigability of effort in the sincere hope of motivating as many as possible to hold their legislatures accountable for bringing the gun issue to the floor for a vote. If they are unable to move with the will of the people, then it's up to the voters to replace them with those who will. The country is at a crossroads with this president who is under investigation for collusion with the Russians and possible obstruction of justice. He is focused on his ego, his business deals, and his friends and will only value the presidency if it was an oligarchy the likes of Russia, North Korea, or China.

There have been numerous presidents gracing the Oval Office over the years, and though I didn't necessarily agree with their policies or stance on major issues, I respected the men who were voted in to represent us as the top world leader. For the first time in my lifetime, I have no respect for the man who currently sits in the Oval Office, who is usually asleep or watching television or at Mar-a-Lago playing golf and winning tournaments that he did not participate in.

This current set of GOP men and women are without conscience, manipulative, and spineless. They are robots and puppets whose strings are manipulated by this implicitly biased perpetrator of a president. This group of selfish politicians prefer politics over purpose. They prefer to choose wrong over right simply to protect their positions and a way of life that has long since passed. They are so afraid to take Trump on for fear of him not supporting them in their state's primary. His name-calling, lack of moral compass, and willingness to lie under any circumstance leave the majority of these misfits as rebels without a cause. *What's at stake here is the fragile soul of America.*

I ask my readers who voted for this president to look deeply at who he has surrounded himself with. Make up your own mind if this individual has truly drained the swamp by adding people to his cabinet the likes of Steve Bannon, Anthony Scaramucci, Rudy Giuliani, Sarah Sanders, etc. Trump has created his own pigpen, and his sows are being fed the slop offered up by Fox News, the NRA, and surprisingly, the religious right. Do you get my point? If you wallow in the mud, you may not be a pig, but you take on piglike characteristics like our Congress has done.

I am not asking that you agree with me; just consider these senseless actions on the part of heartless men and women who have traded their hearts and souls for a leader who cares nothing about anything or anyone, including them, if you refuse to wear the Trump insignia.

To the young voting populace out there who felt that they didn't have a candidate who met their expectations and decided to sit the election out, now they see the result. Even though you may feel that one or the other candidate is not your choice, not voting has consequences as you can now see. An individual who chooses not to vote is still a vote nevertheless, and it could allow the lesser of the candidates to win as in this latest election.

It would have been great to have had a third choice, but as of now, the third party options are not viable in challenging the established parties labeled the Democrats and the Republicans. One candidate in a race will represent you whether you like them or not, so it would be plausible to take the high road and vote for the candidate who will meet some of your expectations versus sitting out without a voice. I meet young people every day who seems okay with not voting. Families who have a history of voting usually influence their children to vote. That doesn't seem to be the case with this new voting block of young people. Whether their parents vote or not, they are okay with sitting out if they don't like the candidate pool.

This election was a surprise even to Trump, a disaster for our allies, and the perfect storm for the country. Just at a time when the country was recovering from a recession that delayed the retirement of many boomers, had us positioned again as a strong world leader, and produced an improving economy, we promoted to the highest office in the land an unworthy egomaniac whose self-promoting and lack of a moral compass can and will lead us down a path of destruction.

The impact of a poor voter turnout this past election just conceivably may have affected the two-party system and the GOP specifically in a way that will change the grand old party for decades if not forever. The question now before the Congress and this president is, Have we lost our moral authority? Partisan politics aside, has common sense given way to power and political aspirations? Do we care more about winning elections than about truth, justice, and the American way of life?

President Obama, in all his eloquence, said it best, "Backlash comes from people who are genuinely, if wrongly fearful of change. More often it's manufactured by the powerful and the privileged who want to keep us divided, angry and cynical because it helps them maintain the status quo, and keep their power, and privilege."

CHAPTER 2

Modern-Day Slavery: A Different Approach

A people that elect corrupt politicians, impostors, thieves and traitors are not victims . . . but accomplices.

—George Orwell

I T'S AS IF 2016 and beyond has become the Wild, Wild West again—terrorism, both domestic and international; police gone wild at the expense of good cops; questions about "The Star-Spangled Banner" and its implications; a political circus leading to the presidency; racial divide; white privilege; education affordability; health-care issues; immigration concerns; nuclear proliferation; gun control; school shootings; and terrorism across the globe.

At the time of my writing this work, this president has shut the government down, affecting over eight hundred thousand federal workers; and his position is, "It can be shut for months and even years until I get what I want." The "what I want" he is referring to is a wall along the southern border. He is pitching a temper tantrum not because it is a case of national security but because it was a campaign promise that has no merit. It has been statistically proven that a wall will not affect terrorism as he claims, and the majority of terrorists who are successful in penetrating our borders tend to come in through the airports across the country.

He uses the threat of gangs and drugs to play to the fears of his base and allow Fox News to determine the direction of his decisions. This president is an egotistical maniac who believes that the Office of the President is beyond reproach. He sees himself to be blameless or faultless on anything that is not consistent with reality show mentality. This president was offered $25 billion for border security by the Democrats with the caveat of having a way to citizenship for the DACA (Deferred Action for Childhood Arrivals) kids. DACA is an American immigration policy that allows some individuals who were brought to the United States illegally as children to receive a renewable two-year period of deferred action from deportation and become eligible for a work permit in the US. To be eligible for the program, recipients cannot have felonies or serious misdemeanors on their records. Unlike the proposed DREAM Act, DACA does not provide a path to citizenship for recipients known as Dreamers.

The policy, an executive branch memorandum, was announced by President Barack Obama on June 15, 2012. The US Citizenship and Immigration Services began accepting applications for the program on August 15, 2012. Anything that has Barack Obama's handprint on it was destined for the scrap pile by this jealous president. The fact that President Obama totally ripped him to shreds at the White House Correspondents' dinner laid heavily on his fragile ego. Becoming president gave Trump the opportunity to strike back, and he has in a big way.

The soul and morality of our country are at stake, readers. The human soul is that part of a person that is eternal—the part that lives on after the body dies and decays. Are we as a nation in the decaying stage? Is our human spirit in a steady decline? Do we really care about one another? Does politics take precedence over country? It seems so in this current environment where right takes a back seat to power and politics. I plan, in this work, to dissect these and other questions in a way that is thought-provoking, factual, and fair.

I can't remember a point in my life's history when racism, sexism, homophobia, narcissistic behavior, gun violence, and divisiveness were as prevalent as in this current political climate. Self-aggrandizement is the foundation of this administration.

Be as critical of past president Obama as you would like, but were these things happening to this magnitude under his watch? Be as anti-Obama as you would like, but you have to admit that he ran a tight ship during what was a very severe economic downturn. The low unemployment numbers and improved economy that Trump had taken credit for came as a result of the tough decisions made during the eight years of the Obama administration.

There is little doubt that this president, more than anything, wants to increase his own power and influence and draw attention to his own self-interests and importance. It is a fact, based on decisions and policies to this day, that President Trump is scaling a mountain of self-interest and superiority and wants his cabinet and the country to bow to and kiss his ring. His heroes are Vladimir Putin from Russia, Xi Jinping of China, and Israel's prime minister Benjamin "Bibi" Netanyahu.

For the first time in recent history and counter to the actions of those preceding him, this president is willing to give Kim Jong-un of North Korea an equal footing on the world stage simply to qualify himself for the Nobel Peace Prize. The summit between President Trump and Kim Jong-un did take place on June 12, 2018, though the result amounted to a photo op for the two dictators. Kim Jong-un, the ultimate dictator and human rights violator, will never denuclearize, having finally the long-term goal or aim of developing a warhead that can reach any point within the continental United States. As of November 2018, there has been no progress made toward denuclearizing in Kim's part, and he is thumbing his nose at the president of the most powerful country in the world. Sad!

This paper summit was a ploy to fool the American people into believing that Trump is the great negotiator as he marketed himself in his book *The Art of the Deal*. North Korea, China, and Russia are obviously pulling all the strings here. Mark my word, they will give Trump just enough in the negotiations to save face with his base. Actually, there will be little substance to any agreement between the two leaders. Our president has his pants down around his ankles and is being seduced by Putin, who I believe has damaging information or tapes that could end this presidency if revealed. I have a strong feeling that Russia has been cultivating this relationship for a significant amount of time, and now they reap the benefits.

It is also quite apparent with this new administration that political lines are drawn stronger than the rights you and I have to a fair, safe, and equitable existence. *Spite* takes precedence over *right*, and political lines and dedication to party are stronger values than doing what's right for the country no matter the consequences. The preamble to the Constitution says "we the people," not "they the government." We are not an oligarchy, though some on the political right would love to be governed in that manner. When we glorify leaders as being strong, controlling, and lethal, we are recognizing this style of leadership is more to our liking than one of the people, by the people, and for the people.

Isn't it eyebrow-raising that policies and strategies that were not supported by the Republican-controlled Senate under the past administration for political reasons are now considered the "right thing to do?" This three hundred and sixty–degree turn came as a result of simply changing the political landscape to a new administration. That new administration has, as a support base, the infrastructure and support of the three branches of government. President Obama's proposals and ideas were rejected primarily because he was a Democrat and he did not have control of the three governing branches. And did I mention he was black? *Yes, I said it.* Having a black man in the White House dug deeply in the annals of hate that still embodies this great country as well as the minds of those having the right to control us through targeted legislation.

Many whom I've had the privilege of discussing President Obama's performance while in office would express how disappointed they were with him. But when pressed on their reasoning, they failed to articulate specifics of their dissatisfaction. They would say, for example, that he had a poor foreign policy record (untrue) or he would not reach across the aisle (another lie) or he was dividing the country (what?). Who has segregated the country by race more than this administration, this president? As far as I am concerned, it's not rocket science to speculate on why. It is demoralizing when a powerful country like ours has struggled mightily to place blacks at an equal level with whites. Many in this country would rather see a person who lacks real ability dawn the White House than have a qualified person of color. Where is your soul, America?

There is still a massa mentality when it comes to people of color and women in power positions in this country. It's hard for me to believe that Hillary, being a women, played heavily in her loss in the past election. White women and white men still, in large numbers, believe that only a white man can be successful as leader of the free world. Again, had it not been for the untimely Comey decision on the emails or the Bernie Sanders base either staying home or voting for a third party candidate, we would have spared ourselves this Armageddon spreading over this country like butter on hot bread. According to the book of Revelation in the New Testament of the Bible, Armageddon is the prophesied location of a gathering of armies for a battle during the end-times, variously interpreted as either a literal or a symbolic location. The term is also used in a generic sense to refer to any end-of-the-world scenario. Armageddon is defined as a dramatic and catastrophic conflict typically seen as likely to destroy the world or the human race. In my estimation, we are one tweet, one button push, one poor decision away from destroying this country as we know it.

This is not supposed to be happening! Why did it happen? It set off a white political backlash that sometimes surprised the political right. Senator John McCain, because of his refusal to bow to the pressures of his own party, has been demonized for doing what he thought was right for the country as it relates to health care, and he refused to play patrician politics on this issue. Unfortunately, on August 25, 2018, John McCain was laid to rest at his beloved alma mater, Annapolis US Naval Academy.

Even in death, McCain was dishonored by Trump by initially lowering the flag to half-mast and raising it a day later. It took the pressure of military groups to cause him to once again lower the flag in honor of the fallen legislator. Then he further dishonored McCain and his family by having Jared Kushner, his son-in-law, and Ivanka, his daughter, attend the funeral when it was clear that John McCain didn't want him or his family in attendance. The swamp just gets deeper and dirtier under this president.

The president made a provocative point during the 2016 election process, referring to McCain being captured as a prisoner of war. He stated something to the effect of, "I don't think he was a hero, a hero doesn't get captured. I respect those who didn't get captured in the first place." This is from a man who used every lie in the book to dodge the draft and never served his country in any military capacity. He will never understand the dedication and sacrifice of a country's hero like John McCain because he will never serve. This president had four (4) college deferments and one (1) for having bad feet, yet he criticized a war hero for serving his country and suffering severe deformities to his body while in captivity.

President Obama was too smart for his own good and wouldn't stay in his place, as would have been expected from those who want to make America great again. So what do they do? They set out to undercut any and everything that he tried to do. Was that placing the country first? I think not. The political right, the red-state voters, created in their mind a fictitious scenario that placed the country in a state of crisis and wondered whether the White House could ever be fumigated. They attacked him politically, attacked First Lady Michelle and her health initiatives, affected his attempt to improve the economy, and tried to block his efforts to deliver much-needed health services to millions under the Affordable Care Act. They fought his attempts toward clean energy and gave him no credit for bringing the country out of what could have been another extended recession. To show the state of following the issues and being informed and educated on what would continue the greatness of this country, many of Trump's followers didn't know that the Affordable Care Act and Obamacare were one and the same. Blacks are the only people who are compared to animals. Think about it!

Senator Mitch McConnell, in an interview with the *National Journal*'s Major Garrett on October 29, 2010, made this statement: "The single most important thing we want to achieve is for President Obama to be a one-term president." The man had not been in office less than two (2) years at that time. Those on the right might say that he was simply playing politics, but I say that it was the conservatives accepting the reality that they had not only lost the White House to the Democrats but they had also lost to a black man, and they would do everything in their power to prevent it from happening again. Well, it did two years later when President Obama was reelected to a second term. How did that work for you, Mr. McConnell? Sad!

Many of my fellow business operatives made it clear what side they were on when they said, "Why don't you give President Trump a chance?" to which I responded, "Did you give President Obama a chance?" That tended to shut the conversation down quickly. In other words, if it's something of importance to them, then we should give it a chance; but if it's not significant to them, then our concerns are not important.

That's not unconscious bias; it conscious racism. It's not easy or satisfying to be the only person who looks like you in a group. As a black man, if I am aggressive, I am considered militant; if I am low-key, then I don't have the fire in the belly to succeed; if I speak well, I am referred to as articulate, a word never used to describe a characteristic of a white person; if I am good at sports, it's because I am a genetic freak; if I go to Harvard, it's because of affirmative action and it concerned them not that I worked my butt off to get there. Folks, this is real stuff, and you can't make this stuff up.

It is not easy being a person of color in America and especially now under this racist regime. I wish we could ask Botham Jean, who was shot and killed while sitting in his own apartment by Amber Guyger, a thirty-year-old white police officer who, in her deposition, wanted us to believe that she mistakenly went to his apartment thinking it was hers. Ask Jean how it is being black in America. To add insult to injury, it was not the officer's apartment that a search warrant was issued—it was the victim's.

This is one of many situations where drugs were used as justification for the actions of the crime. We saw this same tactic on the part of the police in the Trayvon Martin case. Making the victim the villain is a newly applied tactic on the part of this administration and those who are paid by our tax dollars to serve. Is this a part of the blue wall of silence? The *blue wall of silence*, also *blue code* and *blue shield*, are terms used in the United States to denote the informal rule that purportedly exists among police officers not to report on a colleague's errors, misconducts, or crimes, including police brutality. If questioned about an incident of alleged misconduct involving another officer, while following the code, the officer being questioned would claim ignorance of another officer's wrongdoing or claim to have no significant information.

In this case of an obvious murder of a young man who was steeped in his religious beliefs, this blue code is trying, in every way, to shift the scenario or use the bait-and-switch method to focus circumstance on this so-called marijuana find (drop) in his apartment versus this obvious negligence and murder by this policewoman. Jeff Sessions, Donald Trump, and the Justice Department have turned a blind eye to these atrocities as they continually turn the clock back on affirmative-action advancements over the past years.

Police culture, or cop culture as it is sometimes called by police officers, has resulted in a barrier against stopping corrupt officers. Police culture involves a set of values and rules that have evolved through the experiences of officers and that are affected by the environment in which they work. From the beginning of their career at their academies, police are brought into this cop culture.

While learning jobs and duties, recruits will also learn the values needed to make it to a high rank in their organization. Some words used to describe these values are as follows: *a sense of mission, action, cynicism, pessimism, machismo, suspicion, conservatism, isolation,* and *solidarity.* The unique demands that are placed on police officers, such as the threat of danger as well as scrutiny by the public, generate a tightly woven environment conducive to the development of feelings of loyalty.

These values are claimed to lead to the code—isolation and solidarity leading to police officers sticking to their own kind, producing an "us against them" mentality. The "us against them" mentality that can result leads to officers backing up and staying loyal to one another; in some situations, it leads to not ratting on fellow officers (Wikipedia).

Yes, this is a regime with a totalitarian leader. In politics, a regime is the form of government or the set of rules, cultural or social norms, etc. that regulate the operation of a government or institution and its interactions with society. You may consider it too harsh to call this government totalitarian, but its definition is scarily similar to what we are experiencing under the current leadership and his supporting administration.

These blue code tactics are indicative of these type of governments.

Totalitarianism is a political concept where the state recognizes no limits to its authority and strives to control every aspect of public and private life wherever feasible. Totalitarian regimes stay in political power through rule by one leader and an all-encompassing propaganda campaign, which is disseminated through the state-controlled mass media, a single party that is often marked by political repression (gerrymandering–the process of setting electoral districts; gerrymandering is a practice that attempts to establish a political advantage for a particular party or group by manipulating district boundaries to create partisan-advantaged districts), personality cultism ("Do as I say, not as I do"), control over the economy (tax cuts for the rich), regulation and restriction of speech (fake news media chants), mass surveillance, and widespread use of terror (immigration regulations).

A distinctive feature of totalitarian governments is an "elaborate ideology, a set of ideas that gives meaning and direction to the whole society." China has been using totalitarianism as a practical way and recently developed a social credit system to screen and rank its citizens based on their personal behavior.

During the campaign, Trump used themes like Make America Great Again and "Lock her up" as related to Hillary Clinton, calling her Crooked Hillary, and labeled the media as fake news when it did not play to his massive need for acceptance. This is exactly how a dictatorship works. A dictatorship is a form of government where a country is ruled by one person or political entity and exercised through various mechanisms to ensure the entity's power remains strong. A dictatorship is a type of authoritarianism in which politicians regulate nearly every aspect of the public and private behavior of citizens.

These definitions bring into clear view what Trump's intentions are during his stay in the White House. He thinks he is an oligarch; he admires dictators and is an authoritarian wannabe. Authoritarianism is a form of government characterized by strong central power and limited political freedoms. Trump has control of the three branches of government and would love to control the scenario around the military, immigration, the wall, and freedom of speech. If a leader has control of the legislative, judicial, and executive branches, he can change the laws to fit his agenda, which falls under the legislative branch; carry out laws in a misinterpreted way as with the border immigration fiasco, which is under the executive branch; and finally, use the increasingly conservative court to turn back the clock on progress in the minority, immigration, and voter regulation areas. We may just have a dictatorship on our hands.

We cannot sell this dictator-like personality short because he is a master of deception and uses mind games to keep his base energized. These chants and themes that are a backbone to his world are mind conditioning and can have a negative effect on the psyche of those who are not as focused on what's best for the country but instead what's best for them personally. If you repeatedly put into the minds of weak-minded people something that you want them to believe, they will, and think it's a great idea as in the slogan "Make America Great Again" or "Lock her up" or "Fake news" or "The media is the enemy." Saying these enough times by someone in a power position causes weak-minded people to parrot what is being said.

The key traits of totalitarianism are a one-party rule with a dictatorship, a dynamic leader, an ideology that sets the goals of the state, and methods of law enforcement that ultimately censor what people can read and watch. Are we headed for either an authoritarian or a totalitarian government? The difference between an authoritarian government and a totalitarian government is not entirely known because even theorists disagree about the two. However, both forms of government use force and often fear to control, with *totalitarian* governments controlling every aspect of people's lives in a way that *authoritarian* governments sometimes do not.

Donald Trump sees power in driving separation between the races. He sees opportunity in seeking to increase the number of voters who feel disenfranchised by the "browning" of America. He wants to strike fear in the hearts of the poor, the downtrodden, the economically deprived, and the immigrants for the purpose of driving them away from the polls. With the "browning" of America, Trump is well aware that he lost the popular vote by a large margin. With the influx of immigrants, that margin will grow because the majority of these individuals tend to vote Democratic, and Mr. Trump and his band of merrymen are doing whatever they can, whether legal or illegal, to stem the flow.

President Trump, Putin's chump, is sly like a fox. If you let your guard down, he will punch you below your defenses. Older people, poor, black, Latino, Asian, women, immigrants—we are, in military terms, in Trump's kill range and are the target of his unhinged wrath. Since Obama pulled down his pants and spanked that cookie of his during the roast at the correspondents' dinner, he has been on a personal vendetta against Obama and anyone who resembles him. The man has thin skin and can give it out and can't take anyone joking at his expense.

As long as this country sees diversity as a flaw, it will be difficult to fulfill our true potential. During my tenure in corporate America, there was a concerted effort to develop mentoring programs for the purpose of helping minorities and females integrate into the business community. Why do *we* need *special* help to integrate and survive in corporate America? Are we flawed? We go to school and prepare just like others, but we are not given the same opportunities as others. Why not make mentoring programs for anyone who needs it, no matter their race, culture, or gender?

These type of programs are dog whistles for minorities and females, warning us that something special has to be done to elevate us to a level of acceptance in the corporate world. This is called unconscious bias. I believe it to be unconscious bias because many of the individuals involved in the process seem to be good people with honorable intentions. These same programs tend to have minorities mentor minorities and women mentor women. A good mentor can mentor anyone no matter the race or gender.

Just recently, hate-based violence happened in Charlottesville, Virginia, where an individual who was a part of the white nationalist rally group used his vehicle to mow down innocent people who were peacefully demonstrating against those who chose violence and hate over diversity and inclusion. There were one dead, nineteen (19) injured, and very little leadership and condemnation of these fascists groups from the leader of the free world–Mr. Trump. Sad! The president's statement, "There are good people on both sides," set the tone for those who would normally do their dirt under the cover of darkness that it was okay to come into the light. On February 14, 2018, a mass shooting occurred at Marjory Stoneman Douglas High School in Parkland, Florida. Yes, it happened within the borders of the United States of America but still no condemnation of the shooter as a domestic terrorist by our president. Seventeen (17) young people were killed and fifteen (15) others were hospitalized, making it one of the world's deadliest school massacres in history. Nikolas Cruz, the man arrested as the shooter, was identified and placed in the custody of the Broward County sheriff department. This was a troubled individual who had given signs in the past of being disturbed, but the signs were left untended.

Hate is like cancer and, if left untreated, will metastasize and eventually affect the entire body. America will pitch a hissy fit and boycott Nike shoes for using Colin

Kaepernick as the face of the company but won't say a word about police killing innocent people on the street or even kids being raped in the Catholic church. These hypocrites were up in arms when Cecil the lion was killed in Africa or when the silverback gorilla was shot to death after a child fell into its enclosure—some thought about the gorilla and not about the safety of the child. Has America lost its soul?

CHAPTER 3

Mass Destruction and the NRA

Yes, people pull the trigger–but guns are the instrument of death. Gun control is necessary, and delay means more death and horror.

–Eliot Spitzer

O N FEBRUARY 14, 2018, a mass shooting occurred at Marjory Stoneman Douglas High School in Parkland, Florida, United States. Seventeen (17) people were killed and fifteen (15) hospitalized, making it one of the world's deadliest school massacres in history. Nikolas Cruz, the man arrested as the shooter, was apprehended and placed in the custody of Broward County sheriff's office. Why didn't we read the signs of this troubled individual, or did we and they were ignored? Why is it always the case that we recognized what we should have done after the fact?

Does law enforcement act or fail to act based on the race of the individuals in question? How many blacks have committed mass murder after their names were placed on a watch list? The data on mass murders in the United States are as follows:

> Whites = 56 or 58 percent
> Blacks = 16 or 16.5 percent
> Latinos = 7 or 7.2 percent
> Asians = 7 or 7.2 percent
> Native American = 3 or 3.1 percent
> Others = 8 or 8.2 percent

It's a matter of preference by the news media, but it's obvious bias when Muslims are called terrorist while others are called unfortunate incidents or mentally ill. An assessment of three recent mass killings has caused a sudden reevaluation of the category of terrorism. There were nine victims at Emanuel African Methodist Episcopal Church in Charleston, eleven people killed by the car in Charleston, and two women murdered at a Louisiana showing of *Trainwreck.* After the Charleston shooting, many were quick to insist the act be defined as terrorism. Well, what else would you call it? For some reason, we tend to save the title of terrorist for Muslims. The soul of America is on trial here, but this current environment of hate seems to take legs under this administration. Say what you want about Obama's administration, but *hate* is not a word that comes immediately to mind as with this administration.

Remember the Columbine High School massacre? It wasn't that long ago and is still vivid in the memory of those still scourged by the death of young minds innocently trying to prepare themselves for what would or could have been a challenging future. It was a school shooting that occurred on April 20, 1999, at Columbine High School in Littleton, an unincorporated area of Jefferson County, Colorado. In addition to the shootings, the vicious and premeditated attack involved a firebomb that would divert firefighters, propane tanks converted to bombs placed in the cafeteria, ninety-nine (99) explosive devices, and car bombs (Wikipedia). The perpetrators, senior students Eric Harris and Dylan Klebold, murdered twelve (12) students and one (1) teacher. They injured twenty (20) and wounded twenty-one (21), and three (3) more were injured while attempting to escape the school. After exchanging gunfire with responding police officers, the gunmen subsequently took the cowardly way out by committing suicide rather than face justice for these crimes against innocent schoolchildren. Where is the outcry from the general public, the clergy, and those on the right concerning this being an act of terrorism? They practically castrated Obama for not saying the words *radical Islamic terrorist*, but they won't call a terrorist act committed by an American an act of terrorism. Why? We know why, don't we?

Let's pause for a moment. Our president and the NRA have convinced their followers that guns are not the problem, and instead, the finger is pointed at the mental illness as the primary culprit. Now come on, man! Mental illness didn't kill those fifteen (15) young people; an AR-15 military-grade weapon did. The AR-15 is not only a fast-firing gun but also highly customizable. There are numerous legal adjustments that can be made to the AR-15's receiver, stock length, sights, handgrip, and even the barrel.

As the *Huffington Post* pointed out, San Bernardino shooters Syed Rizwan Farook and Tashfeen Malik were able to alter the AR-15 to have a larger magazine and to function like a fully automatic, military-style weapon. Why do we, in the greatest country in the world, need weapons of mass destruction on our streets? You don't need a machine gun to kill a rabbit. Gun enthusiasts want you to believe that hunting and family protection are their goals. Do we need AR-15s for target practice on a gun range? I think not! America has lost its soul, the essence and embodiment of the true meaning of the Constitution.

I am a Vietnam War veteran and have guns that have never been fired since I left the war. I clean them, keep them from corroding, but have not had them out of their cases even to do target practice. I have enough other security devices around like outside motion lighting, indoor and outdoor cameras, indoor motion detectors, double security locks on my doors, and a perimeter surveillance system. There has been no need to use my weapon in the fifty-plus years since using them in Vietnam. Now maybe that has not been your experience, and I get that, but sometimes, you have to check what vibes you are sending to others that make you believe that you are in need of not only a single-shot weapon but also an AR-15. Just something to think about.

Something is wrong with our justice system when it's easier to get a gun into school than it is a backpack. I would gladly give up my guns if we had stronger gun laws. If we make it difficult for people who are underage, mentally ill, have a prior felony, or have history of violence to get their hands on these weapons by screening and regulatory laws, we can get a handle on these mass murders. If you park a police cruiser unattended on the highway, people will instinctively slow down because of the implied authority. If we place more limitations on who can purchase a weapon and even more limitations on having the ability to acquire weapons that have the mass destructive ability, we would be in a better place. If individuals knew that violation of laws related to automatic weapons was a felony, there would be more caution taken.

A weapon should be the last line of defense in self-protection. Over seven thousand children are hospitalized or killed due to gun violence every year according to a new study published in the medical journal *Pediatrics*. An additional three thousand children die from gun injuries before making it to the hospital, bringing the total number of injured or killed adolescents to ten thousand each year.

Many studies led by researchers at the Yale School of Medicine highlight the toll gun violence has on child mortality rates in the country. With this type of statistics available to them, why do you suppose our Congress won't act? Is it because it's not their kids, or is it that they care more for their NRA and their strange relationship with Trump than they do for the children of this country? "This study reinforces what we know from the mortality data," Daniel Webster, the director of the Johns Hopkins Center for Gun Policy and Research, told NBC News. "We have an extraordinary health burden in our youth associated with firearms injuries." Firearms are glorified by the adults, who are the greatest influence on these young people. Wake up, America. This problem is bigger than Trump and the NRA. Our children's future is at stake.

According to a report written by Upshot's reporters Kevin Quealy and Margot Sanger-Katz, this level of violence makes the United States an extreme outlier when measured against the experience of other advanced countries. Around the world, those countries have substantially lower rates of deaths from gun homicide. In Germany, being murdered with a gun is as uncommon as being killed by a falling object in the United States. About two people out of every million are killed in a gun homicide. Gun homicides are just as rare in several other European countries, including the Netherlands and Austria. In the United States, two per million is roughly the death rate for hypothermia or plane crashes.

In Poland and England, only about one out of every million people dies in gun homicides each year—about as often as an American dies in an agricultural accident or falling from a ladder. In Japan, where gun homicides are even rarer, the likelihood of dying this way is about the same as an American's chance of being killed by lightning–roughly one in 10 million. Some statistics show that there are approximately thirteen thousand gun homicides in the United States, of which 10 percent is attributed to some form of mental illness, so why would our president point the finger at the mentally ill population rather than the 90 percent others who commit homicides? We know why–he is in the pocket of the NRA.

What is it about the United States that causes law-abiding citizens to feel as if they need not only a gun but also multiple weapons with capabilities of mass destruction? Is it the fear of not being able to protect the family? Is it the sheer idea of sport shooting? Does the weapon give you a feeling of power? Is it fear of those who don't look like you? Is it racism? Is it the fear of the unknown? Truly, what is it? Only you can answer that question.

Nothing rings clearer to the consciousness of a subject than a true example. While having lunch at work with one of the fellow employees, a discussion ensued around guns and gun safety. The individual was a long-tenured employee and a leader in the organization. He was also an avid gun enthusiast who attended gun shows all over the country.

I was the vice president of human resources for the operations side of a major business and had mentored a certain individual over a period to help him with his lack of people leadership skills. He was a white male who obviously had some issues with diversity but felt comfortable being around me because of the rapport that had developed between us over time. Because I was at the executive level in the organization, many of my white brothers and sisters saw me as tolerable. I didn't or don't want to be tolerated; I wanted to be respected. This individual felt comfortable enough around me to let his guard down on some of his deep, dark feelings.

As the conversation advanced into the rights to bear arms, he made a very startling offer to me. He had just returned from a gun show in Texas where he had purchased twelve automatic weapons. He, feeling that I was one of the good black folks, offered me two of the weapons because he knew I had been in the military and, after all, felt that I was "one of the good ones." I asked why he had a need for so many guns. His answer shocked me. He said, "Obama wants to take away our rights to own a gun, and by god, it would be over my dead body. He is a worthless *sob*!" The man's face turned red as a beet. A lot of the pent-up hate started to surface. I obviously hit a nerve, but backing away from a teaching opportunity is not my modus operandi.

I refused his generous offer while removing myself from his company. He could see that I was not supportive of his outburst. His chin dropped to his chest, and I could tell that even he felt that his comments were a bit over-the-top. As I stood to leave, I couldn't let the conversation end without telling him my reason for the refusal of his offer and my displeasure with his comments. I explained to him that I had no need for an automatic weapon and didn't understand his need for one either. I also expressed my support for President Obama and regretted his need to use profanity when referring to the president. As our conversation progressed, there was no sign of an apology, nor did I expect one at that point. His parting words to me was, "Didn't mean to upset you, but there will be a war coming if Obama tried to take away our guns, and I am not the only one who feels that way." I knew he was right, and there are so many others who harbor those sentiments. These type of attitudes and behaviors are indicators of an America that is losing its soul.

I realized what type of personality I was dealing with and immediately cut ties with him. This was obviously a troubled individual, and I felt the need to report this to the CEO, who placed this employee on the watch list. The individual's erratic behavior was finally the last straw, and he was terminated from the company several incidents later. I personally don't have an issue with the Second Amendment. I think individuals should have a right to a gun for hunting, range shooting, and family protection, but I draw the line with those needing weapons of mass destruction.

We are quick in this country to condemn the radical Islamic terrorist, but there is not a word to condemn domestic terrorist hate groups, such as the Ku Klux Klan, white nationalists, the alt-right, or neo-Nazi parties. I guess we give domestic terrorists a mulligan. The flag of hatred and bigotry has been raised to its highest point on the flagpole under this current administration. It seems that the attitude of the white supremacists is to normalize hate and discrimination in this country. I call this period the Trump-a-for-cation of America. It's becoming an administration that has no feelings toward children, people of color, and other people of difference. That's the dog whistle, "Let's make America great again." It's becoming clear what that really means to him and some of his followers.

Political and NRA-based supporters are driving a wedge between blacks and whites, Democrats and Republicans, women and sexism, gay and straight, the powerful versus the powerless. Number 45 has taken over the Republican Party and moved further and further away from its conservative values. What has happened to the grand old party of family values? The party seems to be allowing bullies like Steve Bannon, President Trump, and the alt-right to establish its footing as direction drivers with more radical views on policing, international relations, DACA, environmental issues, and the justice system as a whole.

The Republican Party just recently failed to condemn Judge Roy Moore, who was reported to be a child molester and who was running to win a seat representing Alabama in the US Senate. Isn't it disheartening that usually vocal Obama critics and leaders like Mitch McConnell, Ted Cruz, Orrin Hatch, and Paul Ryan are tongue-tied in condemning the antics of someone like Roy Moore as well as this president whom they know is a danger to democracy as we know it? From his tariffs on goods coming into the country to his attacks on Amazon because he dislikes its owner or his refusal to condemn

Russia for meddling in our country's infrastructure, this president continues to show that he is well over his head in these deep political waters. What we are seeing is not simply a spike in the activity as a result of this new inexperienced administration but instead a new reality that could have dangerous results for people of color as well as for the country. This has been happening in cities across our country, especially those with large minority populations.

CHAPTER 4

A Difficult Time in America's History

If you're going through hell, keep going.

—Winston Churchill

I CLEARLY REMEMBER Theophilus Eugene Connor (July 11, 1897–March 10, 1973), historically known as Bull Connor, an American politician and, without a doubt, a racist who served as an elected commissioner of public safety for more than twenty years in the city of Birmingham in the state of Alabama. He was a thorn in the side of the activities of the American civil rights movement in the 1960s. Under the city commission government, Connor had responsibility for administrative oversight of the Birmingham Fire Department and the Birmingham Police Department.

During this time, Connor legally enforced racial segregation and denied civil rights to black citizens, especially during the Southern Christian Leadership Conference's Birmingham campaign of 1963. He became an international symbol of institutional racism throughout the South. Bull Connor directed the use of fire hoses and police attack dogs against civil rights activists; child protestors were also subject to these attacks. National media broadcasted these tactics on national television, horrifying much of the nation. The outrages served as catalysts for major social and legal change in the Southern United States and contributed to passage by the United States Congress of the Civil Rights Act of 1964 (Wikipedia).

What really happened in Birmingham, Alabama, during the difficult period of Jim Crow and the ironfisted rule of Bull Connor during the '80s? These were suffocating times for those seeking a better life for their families.

Blacks, who were the predominant minority culture at the time, were slowly moving from the grips of backbreaking agricultural jobs to jobs in foundries and mills all over the South. But this Jim Crow period reminds me so much of what is happening today. Jim Crow was an era in which whites, mostly but not always in the South, used methods, sometimes legal, sometimes illegal, often deadly, but always immoral, to maintain political and cultural domination and control over blacks.

Our forefathers and foremothers were reduced to second-class citizenship, and laws were written to sustain that humiliation. Our people were denied the right to vote, kept separate from whites in most phases of life, and in general, treated as if we were subhuman in an effort to justify white supremacy and keep the black population under tight control. We always lived on the other side of the tracks.

Now there seems to be a new Jim Crow period–the period under the Trump administration, which is behaving eerily like those of the Bull Connor era. It seems that many in the majority culture have fears that with open borders and an influx of new immigrants into the country, "their control and way of life is being threatened." Immigration was a means to an end for those facing rape, murder, castration, and incarceration.

According to David Stringer, a Republican lawmaker in Arizona, "If we don't do something about immigration very, very soon, the demographics of our country will be irrevocably changed and we will be a very different country. It will not be the country you were born into." I am sure that statements like that of Mr. Stringer will assist us in making America great again. How can anyone in a leadership position, as Mr. Stringer is, place the ills of the country on the growth of immigrants? I would love to have Mr. Stringer espouse which immigrant groups he is referencing, but I think we can all guess which ones he references. Statements like these and others made by Donald Trump do not signify a desire for social justice.

I am one who believes in securing the borders but not based on the origin of the immigrants. Our borders seem to be closed to Mexicans, Africans, Filipinos, and other people originating from brown-skin countries. If that doesn't tug at your heartstrings, then what about the children who are being placed in camps and separated from their parents simply because the parents, as immigrants, are fleeing gangs, poverty, and rogue governments and seeking a better quality of life for their children? To have a baby snatched from the breast of a woman with no means of security or bonding simply to satisfy a law was not intended for the current interpretation.

Our justice department, under the directions of Jefferson Beauregard Sessions III, even went as far as quoting scripture from the Bible to justify his actions. How shameful can one be? If he had read further, he would have known the true meaning of that scripture. The political manipulators have historically used the Bible as a weapon and are citing it as a means to dehumanize others or to justify atrocities committed in the name of God and country. They were simply moralistic morons who played on the religious fears of the public.

The current Trump administration is guilty of some of the most horrendous and egregious violations of human rights ever experienced in our lifetime, and it would have its evangelical constituency believe that all the horror it imposes is the will of God. That, in their minds, plays to the religious base. The less they know, the easier they are to influence. The scripture that Sessions quoted was Romans 13:1–7.

According to a comprehensive report by CNN on the statement related to this Bible teaching, Attorney General

Jeff Sessions, on Thursday, instructs Christians to submit to "God's servants." What he really meant was, submit to this rogue government. The Bible passage states, "Let everyone be subject to the governing authorities, for there is no authority except that which God has established." The passage goes on to say, "The authorities that exist have been established by God. Consequently, whoever rebels against the authority is rebelling against what God has instituted, and those who do so will bring judgment on themselves."

It gives me chills that Sessions and others like him prostitute the intentions of the Bible and God's Word for their personal gratification. These individuals, in more cases than not, never grace the doors of the church until there is a photo op. According to a CNN report, Romans 13 has been cited by Nazi sympathizers, apartheid enforcers, slave owners, and loyalists opposed to the American Revolution. Modern Christians have wrestled with how to apply the passage to issues like abortion, same-sex marriage, and taxes but leave it to Trump and Sessions to make it clear for all of us.

Many politicians, like Mr. Stringer and our president, long for a period in which things were separate but terribly unequal. Under Jim Crow, these unequal laws were revered by those in power and were a detriment to those not in power but are the recipients of these shameful interpretations of the law.

Separate but equal was a legal doctrine in United States constitutional law that justified and permitted racial segregation as not being in breach of the Fourteenth

Amendment to the United States Constitution. It guaranteed equal protection under the law to all citizens and other federal civil rights laws. Under this doctrine, as long as the facilities provided to each race were equal, state and local governments could require those services, facilities, public accommodations, housing, medical care, education, employment, and transportation be segregated by race, which was already the case throughout the former confederacy.

Jim Crow laws were state and local laws enforcing racial segregation in the Southern United States. Enacted after the Reconstruction period, these laws continued in force until 1965. They mandated racial segregation in all public facilities in states of the former Confederate States of America, starting in 1890 with a "separate but equal" status for African Americans. African Americans turned to the courts to help protect their constitutional rights, but the courts challenged earlier civil rights legislation and handed down a series of decisions that permitted states to segregate people of color.

In the well-documented and pivotal case of *Plessy v. Ferguson* in 1896, the US Supreme Court ruled that racially separate facilities, if equal, did not violate the Constitution. Segregation, the Court said, was not discrimination. Separate but equal doctrine refers to a now-defunct principle that allowed African Americans to be segregated if they were provided with equal opportunities and facilities in education, public transportation, and jobs. The rule was expounded in the case *Plessy v. Ferguson* (US 1896), where the court held that if one race is inferior to the other socially, the Constitution of the United States cannot put them upon the same plane.

The object of the Fourteenth Amendment was undoubtedly to enforce the absolute equality of the two races before the law, but in the nature of things, it could not have been intended to abolish distinctions based upon color or to enforce social, as distinguished from political equality, or a commingling of the two races upon terms unsatisfactory to either.

This ruling was overruled by the court in *Brown v. Board of Education* (US 1954), where the court held that "segregation with the sanction of law, therefore, has a tendency to retard the educational and mental development of African American children and to deprive them of some of the benefits they would receive in a racially integrated school system. In the field of public education the doctrine of 'separate but equal' has no place. Separate educational facilities are inherently unequal. Therefore, segregation is a deprivation of the equal protection of the laws guaranteed by the Fourteenth Amendment."

Being a part of the baby boomer generation, I lived through those times, and it was definitely separate, and there was nothing equal about it. Our schools were substandard, and our books were of poor quality and were hand-me-downs from the white schools. Many of the books were tattered and torn, and pages were missing from many of the chapters. How can things be equal when research data is missing and, in many instances, it was difficult to find the inevitable conclusion of the research?

We could only use selected sports stadiums whenever the white schools were not using them. We had no band rooms or labs on our campuses. The only skills learned, beyond the normal curriculum, was tailoring, art, or home economics—nothing that effectively prepared us for the new technology revolution. The playing field was not only not leveled but was also tilted toward injustice.

Public water fountains were labeled "colored" and "white" when they were right next to each other. Did the water taste different? Did it originate from a different source? Public toilets were labeled the same, as if even our waste was different. We, as kids, always thought that the water coming from the fountains marked as white was sweeter and tasted better than our water, but we were too afraid to cross the line and sample it. We did the best we could with what we had, and yes, we are still standing. Separate but equal was a joke, but it was the law of the land.

When integration did finally release the choke hold on our communities, it was not always in our favor. In our black schools, there were strong relationships developed between the school and the homes. The black teachers cared about us personally and were extensions of our parents. Students didn't skip class much because there were truant officers roaming the community seeking those who were playing hooky, as how we called it in those days. They, the school system, had our best interest at heart and knew that education was the way out of our economic conditions and the poverty that was a way of life and not a mental focal point. The personal attention given to the students in our black schools came to an abrupt end in many black communities under the new integration order.

The personal touch was nonexistent from many of the white teachers. I am sure it was hard to care when their overall opinion of us was of second class. The relationship between the home and school was strained, and the teachers were merely going through the motions of teaching black kids that they had no connection with or real interest in whether they succeeded. The only connection parents had to the school was through PTO, PTA, or parent / student-teacher meetings. In many of the meetings (PTO/PTA), our parents were outnumbered by the majority class and would have little to say for fear of reprisal. Economically, most black families depended on having both parents work to pay the bills, so many of us were latchkey kids.

This administration's motto is "Make America Great Again." At what point in history is Mr. Trump referring to? America is already great and has been for a long time, so what did he mean? Was it during the Jim Crow period that he relishes? Was it slavery? I would love to have him define when America was great in his mind. This man has convinced his followers that coal is clean and will make a comeback; he thinks that racist organizations–like the Aryan Nations, the Ku Klux Klan, and the skinheads–are good people, that immigrants are rapist and murderers, that all news that don't agree with him is fake news, that women are toys to play with, and that the military is his play toy and power base.

This is a president who wants to see tanks and military force paraded down Pennsylvania Avenue as the oligarchs do in China, Russia, and North Korea. The last parade of the sort, held by George Bush, cost in excess of $12 million, and that was in 1991. You can double that amount in today's costs for such a parade. And for what? To satisfy the ego of this president and his zeal for ultimate power? It's a continuation of his desire for Putin-like power as well as having the military kiss his ring for appointing many of them to key cabinet posts. How is that working for him?

Going back in time, there was the terrible incident in Los Angeles California where Rodney King, a taxi driver, became internationally known after a tape was released of him being beaten on March 3, 1991, by Los Angeles Police Department officers following a high-speed car chase. A witness, George Holliday, videotaped much of the beating from his balcony and sent the footage to local news station KTLA. The footage shows four officers surrounding King, several of them striking him repeatedly, while other officers stood by. Parts of the footage were aired around the world and raised public concern about police treatment of minorities in the United States.

Another of these atrocities was the 1967 Detroit riot, also known as the 12th Street riot or the 1967 Detroit rebellion, which was the bloodiest race riot in the five-year wave of violence known as the "long, hot summers of

1964-68." Composed mainly of confrontations between black people and police, it began in the early morning hours of Sunday July 23, 1967, in Detroit, Michigan; it was one of 159 such riots in the "Long, hot summer of 1967". The precipitating event was a police raid of an unlicensed, after-hours bar known as "The Blind Pig", on the city near west side. It exploded into one of the deadliest and most destructive riots in American history, lasting five days and surpassing the violence and property destruction of Detroit's 1943 race riot just 24 years earlier.

Then there were the King assassination riots. The 1968 Chicago riots were sparked in part by the assassination of Martin Luther King. Dr. King was shot while standing on the balcony of his room at the Lorraine Motel in Memphis, Tennessee, on April 4, 1968, where he was supporting the garbage workers. During that same period, over one hundred major US cities experienced disturbances, resulting in roughly $50 million in damage.

Now what do you think was the identifying thread that ran through each of these events at its core? Correct, it was large cities with large minority populations and high unemployment and poverty. This country has, for decades, turned a blind eye to poverty and depressed communities through minimum wage laws and gerrymandering. In the process of setting electoral districts, gerrymandering is a practice that attempts to establish a political advantage for a particular party or group by manipulating district boundaries to create partisan-advantaged districts. The resulting district apportionment is known as a gerrymander.

Then there was voter depression, which is "alive and well" in this current political environment. Those wishing to eliminate voters in large-minority districts used tactics such as requiring unreasonable identification for older citizens, changing voter districts, closing polls early, changing voter locations at the last minute, and purging voter rolls. Since 2008, states across the country have passed measures to make it harder for Americans—particularly black and brown people, the elderly, students, and people with disabilities—to exercise their fundamental right to cast a ballot. According to Think Progress, the American News Process,

> "Democratic turnout could drop by an estimated 8.8 percentage points in general elections when strict photo identification laws are in place," compared to just 3.6 percentage points for Republicans.

According to the Plum Line news, President Trump has shut down the commission he had appointed to examine voter fraud, which is good news. Its true purpose was to spread misinformation and justify further Republican vote suppression efforts. But don't think for a moment that the GOP is done trying to make it harder for people to vote, particularly people who might be likely to vote for Democrats. That effort is still in effect, and it'll be looking for new ways to use the power of the federal government to advance it.

This book will hopefully educate readers on how far we had come before the Trump-a-for-cation of America.

The Republican Party has been hijacked by Trump, and it seems that there is nothing they can do about it. Voices like Mitch McConnell, Paul Ryan, Kevin McCarthy, Cathy Rogers, John McCain, and others have been hushed by the tactics of this new reality under Trump. Though McCain has challenged the administration at key junctures, he withered in the end to vote along party lines for legislation that they knew would benefit only the top 1 percent of the country as with tax reform.

These Republican leaders vote along party lines for fear of backlash from this president when things don't go his way. With the 2018 midterm approaching, only the Republicans who had not planned to run were willing to step out on faith and speak their mind. Those up for reelection seem to have "Trump-itis." As was true during the election, Trump would label his opponent with catchy titles that would stick throughout the campaign, such as Crooked Hillary (Clinton), Little Marco (Rubio), Lying Ted (Cruz), Low-Energy Jeb (Bush), Crazy Bernie (Sanders), and Goofy Elizabeth or Pocahontas (Warren).

As simple as this tactic seemed, it was effective in getting into the minds of the voters. Calling Hillary crooked had a behind-the-scenes effect on those who were on the fence. Many of the millennial voters whom I had conversations with felt that neither candidate deserved their vote. They were tired of the Clintons and felt that Trump was unqualified. These ideas left an opening for Trump's followers and the deplorables, as Hillary labeled them, to sweep Trump into the presidency.

I refuse to label all of Trump's voters as deplorable, but all deplorables, I do believe, voted for Trump, who, in his first year as president, has attacked every group that doesn't look like him. Think about what was said about Puerto Ricans after the hurricane, other Latinos, blacks, Africans, Indians, and others from brown and black countries. Those who chose to support this man must realize now that he is not representing all Americans with his elimination of all things related to supporting the black and brown people and creating legislation that benefits the rich over the poor and middle class. Over eight hundred thousand people could be deported if the immigration laws are not ratified. According to the report, between August 15, 2012, and March 31, 2014, there were 553,197 applications approved, 69,177 still under review, and 20,311 denied.

America has been a country that opened its arms to those who were looking for a better life. This country was built and developed from the skills and sweat of immigrants, but all of a sudden, the new sheriff in town wants to rewrite the Constitution. This president only has to roll over in his bed and see that there is an immigrant lying next to him in the form of Melania. Sorry, my mistake—he has to go down the hall and up the stairs because they sleep in separate rooms. Sad! Redaction is in order for this administration after just one year of Armageddon.

CHAPTER 5

Trump's Appraisal

Empty minds make the most noise.

—Plato

D ONALD JOHN TRUMP is the forty-fifth president of the United States, elected on January 20, 2017. In addition to now masquerading as a politician, he is a successful business magnate and television personality. I never thought that I would say this, but our president, who holds the most influential and powerful position in the world, is truly a racist. He is, has been, and always will be.

Whenever a strong statement of that nature is made, it has to be accompanied with facts. In 1973, his family real estate business was sued by the Justice Department only to settle out of court without having to admit guilt. The company was required to take some nondiscriminatory steps. It was nothing more than a slap on his small hands. Then his weekly rhetoric about those who look nothing like him and him taking every opportunity to prop up those who do show his racist gene.

In 1991, Trump stated in his book *Trumped!* how he hated having black guys count his money. He continued on stating that the only kind of people he wants counting his money are short guys who wear yarmulkes. Then in 1989, he took out a four-page ad entitled "Bring Back the Death Penalty. Bring Back Our Police." In that piece, he spoke about roving bands of wild criminals. Now who do you think he was referring to? Five black and Latino individuals were convicted and later released for the rape of a white woman. This ad, calling for the reinstatement of the death penalty, grew out of his deep-rooted feelings that his idea of what society is supposed to be had to be protected. He and his business took out $85,000 worth of ads in three major news sources to spread his hate. In the advertisement, Donald says that Mayor Edward I. Koch wanted hate removed from their hearts. Trump wanted to hate these muggers and murderers, and he did. He said that they should be forced to suffer and, when they kill, should be executed for their crimes. Trump went on to say in the article that a well-educated black had an advantage of a well-educated white in terms of the job market. What is wrong with this man who many of our uninformed voters chose to place in the Oval Office? Has the country lost its souls, integrity, and moral compass?

As the son of a wealthy real estate developer, Trump attended the Wharton School at the University of Pennsylvania before taking over as head of the family business. He attended Fordham University for two years before transferring to the Wharton School at the University of Pennsylvania. Given that there were approximately 366 listed 1968 Wharton graduates on QuakerNet, Penn's alumni database, the dean's list of fifty-six students represented approximately the top 15 percent of the class. The fact that Trump's name was nowhere to be found suggests that his academic record at Penn was not as outstanding as he had claimed, according to a report written by Alex Rabin and Rebecca Tan.

After graduating in 1968 with a bachelor of science in economics and concentration in finance, he joined his father's real estate company. Between 1966 and 1968, it's more than a coincidence that none of the students at Wharton during this time have any recollection of him. You would think that someone as public as he and his family are would have been remembered for something that he did.

After taking over a business built by his father, he built and renovated numerous hotels, casinos, and office towers during his business career, accumulating a net worth of billions. He also owned several beauty pageants and ventured into reality television as well. Expanding his egotistical aspirations, he decided to feed that huge ego by dabbing into politics in the early 2000s and setting his eyes on the presidential office more for the publicity than seeing himself as a serious candidate.

According to conservative news reports, enough voters were pushed into the Trump camp by the prior administration's efforts to reverse traditional discrimination against blacks and women. This included the increasing diversity of American society and a projected future when whites will be in a minority, by the fact that Democrats had produced a black president and a female presidential candidate. As much as we would like to think that this is a new day and that radical racist ideas are far and few from the old days, we find ourselves heavily involved in chasing the racist tornadoes of this administration and those who will blindly follow it without question.

As a celebrity, Trump's career was marred by allegations of sexual misconduct, and he also earned much criticism for his extravagant lifestyle and controversial comments on immigrants from Islamic nations. Despite the controversies surrounding him, Trump ran for the 2016 presidential election as a Republican, won the nomination from seven other candidates, and defeated Democratic candidate Hillary Clinton in a shocking and unexpected victory.

Donald Trump is the first person to assume presidency without prior military or government service, and at seventy, he is also the oldest person to assume the office. You can't run a company without experience, nor can you operate on a patient or try a case in court without being a doctor or lawyer, so why is it that there was so much confidence in his base that he was fit to be president with what is at stake in the world political and socioeconomic arena? Many would counter that Obama had little to no political experience, but President Obama had the maturity of a leader. His most recent job before being elected president was being a US senator representing Illinois. Prior to that, he was a community organizer and an advocate for the poor, he was a civil rights attorney, he was a law school professor, and finally, he was an Illinois state senator.

Many in America strongly believe that Trump is racist, according to a February Associated Press-NORC Center for Public Affairs Research poll. The poll says that six of ten people have that belief. And those numbers increase when controlled for people of color. More than eight in ten blacks and three-quarters of Hispanics think that Trump is racist. So why do the majority of white supporters don't? Is it the unconscious bias of the racist gene? Just asking.

These statistics were present prior to Trump stumbling into the White House. He has historically promoted policies that were adverse to people of color. The voters knew this prior to the election but still voted for this celebrity. When Trump called Mexican immigrants rapists and murderers during his campaign announcement speech, that communicated to many Americans–including white supremacists–that Trump's vision of a great America did not include a diverse America. The scariest part of this ideology is there are many who agreed with him.

Since his election by the Electoral College, Trump has proven that you can't teach an old racist dog new tricks. These events listed below have given energy to social deviants, like David Duke, and they hope that the president shares their vision of making America great again, including the following:

> The violent protests in Charlottesville after the Unite the Right rally and Trump's blaming of both sides in his response
> The administration's slow response to Hurricane Maria, which led to the estimated deaths of thousands in Puerto Rico
> The ban on citizens from several majority-Muslim countries in Africa and the Middle East from entering the United States
> The numerous calls from white citizens reporting blacks for working while black, jogging while black, barbequing while black, swimming while black, sleeping in a common area of a dorm while black
> The labeling of the countries that send black immigrants to the United States as shithole countries
> The arrest and separation of children from their parents at border crossings with no plan of how to reunite these families

One of the best quotes of a Trump supporter that I have found is this: "He will sucker in talent, tell them that their work is terrible, push them to achieve beyond what they think is possible, and then take credit for their successes as he tells America, and the world, that their projects are the best thing that has ever happened. This tactic, to this point, has worked and united his base. It's not pretty, but it works."

As we continue to populate President Trump's scorecard, and it pains me to address him as such, let me give you one man's opinion before I launch off into a world of euphoria that will be factual, depressing, and downright demoralizing. In the 2016 election, where President Trump so skillfully and convincingly wrestled the presidency from Hillary Clinton, who, by most calculations, had the election in the bag, the following situations caused a disappointing change of events.

The fall from the political mountain started for Hillary when many started to question her health fitness for office after she collapsed while campaigning. Well, who was there to plant the seeds of doubt but old Donald J. Trump. He proved to be a master at exploiting the weaknesses or lapses of his opponents. He is a master in turning a liability into an asset. He started to label her as medically unfit to serve while continuing to paint her image as Crooked Hillary, relating to the emails, her foundation, and Benghazi. He even simulated hitting her with a golf shot while she was boarding a plane and was never held accountable. There were those infamous emails that, because of the numerous investigations by the Justice Department, cost the US taxpayers enough to fully finance those needing coverage under the Affordable Care Act.

Next came the untimely or timely, whichever side of the political spectrum you happen to be on, announcement by the director of the FBI, James Comey, concerning the need to reopen the email trilogy because some emails were found to be on a separate computer of Huma Abedin, the wife of Anthony Weiner. Several emails with classified information from Hillary's aide, Abedin, were among a tranche of documents released that were found on Anthony Weiner's personal computer during an FBI probe. Comey couldn't seem to decide whether he wanted to do the right thing involving the email controversy by staying silent until after the election or support his conservative views and release them, knowing the potential impact.

Just in the twenty-fifth hour when it was certain that Hillary Clinton was on the verge of becoming the first female president, the rug was snatched from under her just as if a tablecloth had been skillfully snatched from a table setting without disturbing any of the place settings on the table. Did he know what impact a bombshell announcement of that nature would have, or was it truly a calculated error on his part? Whichever you choose to believe, it set Hillary's campaign, which was losing steam anyway, on a downward spiral that would never give her a chance to recover as the campaign was in its final stage.

Though I believe Comey to be a professional FBI leader who has integrity, I must say, that was playing partisan politics with the last-minute move against Hillary. I must believe that he regrets his actions now as this drama has played itself out. His politics and political views tended to overwhelm the moment in a very critical stage of the campaign and had, in my view, created enough doubt in the minds of those on the fence to not vote at all or to vote for Trump or a third party.

CHAPTER 6

Russia's Influence on Our Elections

We live in a world where finding fault in others seems to be the favorite blood sport. It has long been the basis of political campaign strategy. It is the theme of much television programming across the world. It sells newspapers, whenever we meet anyone our first, almost unconscious reaction may be to look for imperfections.

–Henry B. Eyring

LET'S CONSIDER HOW and why there was this major collapse of Hillary Clinton at the end of a long and lackluster campaign. It was evident, to those of us standing on the outside, that the email fiasco was first drummed up by Donald Trump when he so skillfully, during the campaign, asked the Russians to find and release any emails of Hillary's. Isn't it a coincidence that he seemed to know just when and how to squeeze the WikiLeaks/Russian toothpaste from its container and just when the campaign was turning in Hillary's direction? I truly believe when all the investigations are complete, you will find that Trump and Russia had a hidden partnership that, if not uncovered, could mean the destruction of our democracy as we know it.

Additionally, as Hillary seemed to regain her footing from some earlier missteps on the campaign trail, she stopped campaigning in the Rust Belt and blue-collar areas, such as Ohio, Pennsylvania, Michigan, and Virginia. Did she think they were solidly in her corner and had no need to further campaign in those areas? She rightfully laid out a vision of clean energy—natural gas, wind, and solar—but, in doing so, lost those in the coal industry by not sharing ideas on how to bridge the skill gap of those who would lose their jobs as innovation embraced the future. Though she was correct in her futuristic look, it was not the opportune time when seeking votes. Mr. Trump seized the opportunity to lie to those voters about his ability to revitalize the industry and save their jobs when he knew he couldn't.

The voting public wanted some form of hope even if it was in the form of a lie. They chose to believe his dishonesty versus realizing, through educating themselves, the coal industry will fail to exist in a few years. Controlling emissions and promoting cleaner energy alternatives were the country's objective prior to this administration's attack on anything touched by Obama.

As far as keeping jobs in this country as well as bringing jobs back to the United States, any moves of that sort were in the works prior to Dishonest Trump taking office. As a businessman in my own right, a person knowledgeable about business strategies and drivers, the market and consumer demands drive these types of decision, not a lying president. If a company sees a competitive edge to produce in other countries, you can bet they will move to those countries where the labor, materials, and transportation costs are lowest. These will always be company bottom-line decisions.

Another pivotal point in the election was when Bill Clinton arranged the ill-timed meeting with Loretta Lynch, then attorney general, which surely raised eyebrows, knowing that Hillary was still under investigation because of the alleged email scandal. Yes, it was a fake scandal because the emails had been scrutinized by very astute people. Had there been a smoking gun, it would have been found and made public. The reincarnation of Benghazi by the Republicans, which became an anvil around Clinton's neck as a result of the loss of American lives in Libya, continued to haunt her campaign, and Trump took advantage of hammering her on sensitive issues at his rallies.

The 2012 Benghazi attack took place on the evening of September 11, 2012. Islamic militants attacked the United States consulate in Benghazi, Libya. Killed in the attack were US ambassador J. Christopher Stevens and Sean Smith, a US diplomat. Though Clinton, in my research, asked and had been denied more support for those protecting our assets in Benghazi, the incident happened on her watch, and the vampires from the political right pounced on the opportunity to stick another pin in the cushion and suck the blood from her struggling campaign. In fact, if there was any blame in this matter, it belonged with the State Department and the intelligence community. When American lives are lost, someone had to be the scapegoat, and it was very craftily laid at her feet by the Republicans. All these events transformed a fairly sure six- to nine-point lead to a slim loss to Trump, who is now the forty-fifth president of the United States. Using Trump's word, sad.

The morning after the election, the country, both domestically and internationally, was in a state of shock. The unthinkable had been accomplished. David had slain Goliath, the chickens had come home to roost, and the cat was out of the bag. As noted writer and teacher Ernest Agyemang Yeboah so skillfully stated, "And just as the game was about to close, he scored a goal to close the game".

As I travel around the country, many in the international communities continue to ask, "What were you Americans thinking to have elected a leader whose brand is tainted with hatred, misogyny, lying, and an obvious lack of domestic and international leadership experience?" The United States has been the template that other countries look up to as the model of how things should be done. We are slowly becoming the brand that others will no longer look up to.

Here is my opinion of the irony of this situation: Donald Trump never wanted the job. He was not in it to win it. He was in it for the publicity of having a place on the world stage for his businesses and that huge ego. His eyes, upon receiving the news of his win, were like the red-and-white rotating cylinders outside of most barbershops. He was as shocked as the rest of us. Now he is the most powerful person on the planet. I believe that he would gladly go back to his playboy lifestyle if his ego would not take a major hit. Even his longtime friend Roger Ailes, prior head of Fox News, didn't believe that Trump had the political savvy to win the election. Many of us went to bed on election night believing that the Donald did not have a snowball's chance in hell to win the presidency. We and the national polls were wrong no matter the influences that affected the election.

I say to you, Mr. President, you are now on the world stage, and you are the main character. Put away your lying and self-grandiosity and be the leader *they* elected. Mr. President, what is your vision? What is your mission? What is your strategic plan for leading the most powerful country in the world? Those who have warmed the seat in the Oval Office before you have maintained our lofty standing on the world stage. Your base is with you now, but what's your next move? How do you lead the most diverse, immigrant-dependent, progressive environment into the near and long-term future? The world is watching.

Mr. President, be careful what you ask for because you just may get it. You had no vision for the presidency, no idea that you would be in charge of the nuclear codes, and no idea that you would have to stand toe to toe with other powerful world leaders and negotiate on behalf of the free world and not just the United States. You had no idea that you would be responsible for the decisions that could affect the well-being of billions of American citizens and allies around the world. You simply wanted to exculpate your reputation and showcase your one-liners, which is obviously a troubling sign of one who needs attention. You're now living in real-time *The Art of the Deal.* Only this time, it's the soul of a country that is at stake and not a business deal. It seems that you came into the Oval Office with your eyes wide shut.

I guess it is human nature that his first inclination was to surround himself with those he trusts—Jared Kushner, Ivanka Trump, two sons Don Jr. and Eric, daughter-in-law Lara, and others. Some have called political malpractice his decision to assign his children and family to top posts in the White House. Ivanka's business dealings internationally and Kushner's and Trump Jr.'s Russian ties may have future implications as Robert Mueller continues his probe into potential collusion and obstruction of justice charges that are being levied against this administration. The president has called the probe into his actions a witch hunt, but I call it the uncovering of one of the largest conspiracies since Watergate. I am convinced that Putin has proof of

Trump's philandering and is using it to pull the strings as a universal puppeteer.

There has been just a few, if any, meetings in a Trump property (the Trump Tower) that have led to as much relentless lying as this infamous rendezvous of June 2016. Three senior members of Donald Trump's presidential campaign—Donald Trump Jr., Paul Manafort, and Jared Kushner—linked up with a Russian lawyer Natalia Veselnitskaya under the express pretense that she would provide them with dirt on Hillary Clinton. Nearly every dimension of the meeting has been spun, mischaracterized, or straight up lied about since. And just recently, it was learned from Natalia that she had direct ties to the Kremlin and Vladimir Putin.

For someone to have gone from Trump Tower and Mar-a-Lago to the White House would be a leap of significant magnitude for one so unqualified. For one so pompous and self-serving to grace the same seat as Lincoln and Roosevelt has unsettled democracies both domestically and abroad. For an individual to be given so much power on one hand and not knowing what the White House is called when asked by a reporter is just sad. It's called the White House, Mr. President!

This president doesn't have the patience for details; he sucks up to dictators from other countries and alienates even some in his own party. It takes a very s-p-e-c-i-a-l person to pull this off, don't you think? Only in America. America will be great again when we get this Putin wannabe out of the Oval Office.

Instead of concentrating on North Korea, China's emergence, and Russia's ambition, Trump is tweeting about his personal egocentric subjects that have little to do with being the commander-in-chief of the most powerful country in the world. His elementary focus is on football players dishonoring the American flag by taking a knee during the national anthem, the size of his crowds at rallies, Hillary's loss in the election, who is loyal to him, and how the FBI is on a witch hunt concerning the Russia probe into their interfering in our elections and his possible involvement with Russia.

Mr. President, if you don't have anything to hide, wholeheartedly support the probe. Cooperate with the investigation; release your taxes as others before you have done. If you do that and you are exonerated from the many allegations, I will have more confidence in your charge that this is all a witch hunt. There should be nothing for Bob Mueller to find out if it's all "fake news." I promise you, Mr. President, if you cooperate and get this behind you, I will give you the chance that many of your deplorable followers are requesting. If not, Mr. President, sir, there must be a volcano behind that smoke that you are blowing up America's rear end.

This president has sent a message to the world that this is his stage now and he is the leading actor. He recently said, "I am the only one that matters." He is correct when there has been no one nor entity having the courage to hold him accountable for fear of reprisal. As stated in earlier chapters, the Republicans in the Senate and House of Representatives, though many disagree with him, are afraid to challenge him for fear of his campaigning against them in the midterm elections. This president is the most dangerous man on the planet because of his power and lack of knowledge in using it. He doesn't listen to those around him who are capable in political matters and continues to make it clear that it's his way or the highway. Even those in the military whom he refers to as his generals are running for the hills. What a mess!

This president is a lot of things: unintelligent, inattentive and impatient for details, racist, bigoted, sexist, unorganized, incompetent, but sly as a fox. He was underestimated by Hillary's campaign, by the pollsters, and even by the American voters. Let's not make that mistake again. America's future depends on it. This president may not be smart in a book sense, but he is cunning, an entertainer, a showman, vindictive; unorganized, and expects loyalty from those under his direction, which makes him dangerous. He seems to want this newfound power to be a dictatorship and/or oligarchy. Anyone who failed to bow down and kiss his ring found themselves tossed out with only what was on their backs. The list is impressive and still growing.

This was not a case of Trump winning but one of Hillary losing, with help from Russia. Had Hillary faced him down when he was stalking her like a wounded animal during the debates, had Comey decided to do the right thing and left the email controversy alone, had Hillary continued to campaign particularly in red and blue states that were considered a toss-up, we would be saying President Hillary today.

I have my own theory as to why Hillary shocked the world by losing to someone who couldn't qualify for a position on her staff. The first part of my theory is many white men believe in the theme "Let's Make America Great Again" because they have more to lose than the rest of us. White men, more than others, had their egos damaged by the loss of the White House to Barack Obama, a black man. That placed the larger percentage of them in the Trump camp. White women are still seething over Hillary's decision to stay with Bill after the Monica Lewinsky ordeal.

Additionally, they have historically served under the leadership of men who looked like them, so that is the standard. Add the majority of them to the Trump camp. More than an expected number of Latinos voted for Trump because of immigration issues. Those who came to this country through the proper channels are resentful of those of their own culture who don't. Additionally, the machismo of Latin men makes it difficult to serve under the leadership of a woman. Black men tend to vote Democratic as a whole, but getting us to the polls is a difficult task. Conversely, black women voted in staggering numbers for Hillary and usually for the Democratic Party. Statistics tends to bare out these assumptions.

Fifty-four (54) percent of college-educated white men voted for Trump. Forty-five (45) percent of college-educated white women voted for Trump. White

Americans make up nearly 70 percent of all eligible voters, and of that enormous group, 63 percent of white men and 53 percent of white women voted for Trump.

Latinos, who did vote, voted overwhelmingly for Clinton. Nationally, Clinton received a record-high 79 percent to 18 percent for Trump, with 3 percent voting for one of the third-party candidates. Although Hispanic males voted in numbers for Clinton, they struggled to vote for a female candidate. Though they are typically alpha males within their environment, they are proud and did not stand for this candidate disrespecting their culture. The male ego can be more dominant and fragile than doing what's best for the country politically, but Latino males and females placed the culture in Hillary's corner. They voted in larger numbers for Trump than expected to the tune of 29 percent.

Sixty-five (65) percent of Asians voted for Clinton, 29 percent for Trump, 4 percent for Libertarian candidate Gary Johnson, and 2 percent for Green Party nominee Jill Stein. East Indian Americans have historically voted Democratic and voted heavily for Barack Obama in 2008 and 2012. In 2016, they voted mostly for Trump. Some speculate that their drastic change came as a result of Hillary's aide, Huma Abedin, being Muslim. Others voted for Trump because of his promise to cut taxes. They were solidly in the Trump camp (Wikipedia).

Trump received approximately 8 percent of the black vote. Many of the young voters whom I personally interviewed were not energized to vote because of the negatives around Clinton and the double negatives around Trump. They were more impressed with Bernie Sanders and his platform of reducing college debt and making college more affordable, criminal justice reform, and affordable health care. So as most can see, a perfect storm was created for Trump. The fact that a large number of millennials who supported Bernie Sanders chose to either set the election out or vote third party, the Comey's emails investigations, Russia's interference, and Hillary's campaign lapses created this perfect tidal wave that swept Trump into the White House.

Over 231 million Americans are eligible to vote. However, based on the early results from the 2016 presidential election, just over 130 million of them voted for either Hillary Clinton or Donald Trump. That being said, over 90 million voters stayed home. In an election that was supposed to see increased voter turnout, fewer Democrats supported Clinton than they did Obama in either 2008 or 2012.

CHAPTER 7

An Increasing Swamp

Nancy Pelosi said that when it comes to cleaning up government, the Democrats have drained the swamp. The only problem with that is what's left after you drain it: Snakes everywhere.
—Jay Leno

THE PRESIDENT MAKES a deal with America to drain what he called the swamp, but it seems after one and a half years in the job, the country made a deal with the devil. The snakes are still there, Mr. President. Charles M. Blow, noted columnist, hit it square on the head when he said, "Concealment makes the soul a swamp. Confession is how you drain it." If confessions are made, Washington would be a ghost town.

President Trump made it clear that he would rather support Roy Moore, the judge from Alabama who ran for the Senate with molestation and sexual harassment charges hanging over his head, than support a Democrat who, in his estimation, would make it hard for him to implement his agenda. There are definitely rodents in this current swamp. Party, self, or country, Mr. President? I think I know which you have and will continue to choose. Is this type of behavior what we are becoming as a country? As a leader goes, so goes the country. In this case, I hope not.

Have we truly lost the soul of America, which is one nation under God with liberty and justice for all? For the president of this country to support the maintaining of statues that have a racist history, support people like Judge Moore, attack professional players who exercise their First Amendment rights, attack talk show host because they don't support his views, attack his own secretary of state who called him a moron, and attack the women who accused him of improperly touching them when he was a private citizen is indicative of what we are becoming as a nation. Our souls, the spiritual or immaterial part of us as humans, are under attack. The swamp is adding a second floor.

President Trump, who has no prior experience in politics, levied vicious attacks on war heroes like John McCain, attacked his own attorney general, Jeff Sessions, for recusing himself from the Russia investigations, talked about women as if they were nothing but sex objects, called blacks who exercise their First Amendment rights sons of a bitch, disparaged Hispanics as rapist and murderers, and placed fault on the people of Puerto Rico for the condition of the island after Hurricane Maria. These are but the tip of the proverbial iceberg of missteps by this administration and its leader, President Trump.

This is a president who has no mental compass. His self-promotions and pompous attitude have the country on the brink of a nuclear war with North Korea and an internal war between the races. He has entered us in a tariff war with China that will cost the American consumer more to maintain the current standard of living. He is being played by China and Russia like a cheap fiddle. The most disturbing aspects of it is, he doesn't know he is being played. Xi Jinping of China and Vladimir Putin of Russia are picking the flesh right off his bones, but he thinks that they are his new sandbox friends. He has developed an international swamp.

China has world dominance as its focus, while Russia is trying desperately to regain its footing as an intimidating world menace. Russia is succeeding as a world bully by interfering in elections across the globe and sewing confusion and doubt in systems that have historically been sound and sophisticated. They, along with WikiLeaks and the Justice Department, have made shambles of our overall election process. Our current administration chooses to believe Putin over US intelligence agencies, whom all have validated their involvement in the 2016 elections.

We speak of unity and togetherness, but the observed actions are counter to the spoken words. Consider these current state of affairs: we have political parties that act as if they are mortal enemies, and we have disrespect of the office of the presidency depending on who is in office. All past presidents, whether you like them or not, represented the position with dignity (with a few exceptions). This current person who sits in the White House has yet to earn the title and respect that goes with the highest office in the land based on his predatory behaviors and erratic and self-promoting behavior–disrespecting immigrants whose blood and sweat assisted in building this great country, categorizing individuals based on the color of their skin instead of the content of their character (Martin Luther King).

A president who disrespects our Gold Star families with his self-aggrandizing attitude and who has launched verbal attacks on war heroes like John McCain, who still wears the scars of captivity, is not a role model for the rest of the world that looks up to us for leadership. I hesitated in playing the race card because that has been obvious with this president. The only two families having issues with the handling of their lost family members were both minority. Consider this so you won't think that I am playing the race card. Consider Trump's Twitter rant and attack on a member of congressional representative Wilson or the personal attention that he gave to the NFL players' protest (the NFL is predominately black) or his personal attention given to ESPN anchor Jemele Hill for criticizing him and the Dallas Cowboys owner, Jerry Jones. Jemelle is black, by the way.

Then there were his attacks on Megyn Kelly, a female Fox News anchor who challenged him with difficult questions during the campaign. Just recently, he was critical of the mayor of San Juan, Puerto Rico, Carmen Yulín Cruz, a female, because she wouldn't kiss his ring and praise him for the truly lousy job being done to help the people of that island after the hurricane. We are over twelve months after the storm at this point, and many parts of the island are still without electricity, while Florida and Texas have recovered because of government support. The one telling fact about Puerto Rico is it is predominately a brown culture but still a part of the United States. Why did we leave these citizens without full access to governmental agencies as was received by Florida and Texas? Just asking the question.

Three GOP senators, Bob Corker of Tennessee, and Jeff Flake of Arizona openly decided not to run again for their seats, calling President Trump untruthful, outrageous, reckless, and undignified. We know about the vicious attack on Arizona senator John McCain, a Vietnam War veteran whom Trump would not call a hero because he was captured when his A-4 Skyhawk jet fighter-bomber was shot down by a SAM (surface-to-air missile) on October 26, 1967. The president stated during the campaign that he only respected soldiers who were not captured (sad). This president has a total of five deferments for school and a medical deferment because of bone spurs in his foot.

Senator John McCain, though I disagree with a lot of his political positions, was a man who served his country in an honorable way, wore the scars of his captors, but still had not earned the respect of a president with a small p who never served at all. I am speaking about this America, the land of the free and the home of the brave, one that I proudly served and defended during the Vietnam War. But I am now very disappointed at how certain segments of our population have no bite of the proverbial pie. I truly think that the media assessment of the image of this president's self-destructive emotional outbursts as a clever political strategy is one that I totally agree with. What this president does is, when caught in a mistake or errant tweet, he cleverly changes the subject to another public interest story. It's called a bait-and-switch tactic.

A bait-and-switch tactic is defined as "the action [generally illegal] of advertising goods that are an apparent bargain with the intention of substituting inferior or more expensive goods." This tactic, which Trump so cleverly integrates into his routine, is considered his bait-and-switch agenda. The strategy encourages listeners to buy into his way of thinking. It makes his base satisfied with the lies and deceit he sells to them as an alternative to a disappointment or inconvenience of his having no plan at all. It suggests that the seller will not show the original product or service advertised (as he has done with those dependent on coal) but instead will demonstrate a more expensive product or a similar product with a higher margin, such as pushing the wall between the United States and Mexico as well as funding for the military as a trade-off.

Trump knew that he couldn't deliver on many of the promises that he made during the campaign but, like many other politicians, live for the glory of the moment. He has all but admitted that his decisions are to play to the base that elected him and not because he believes in his ability to deliver on his promise. He knew that getting Mexico to pay for the wall was a lie, but it was what his base wanted to hear. He knew that it would not be easy to repeal Obamacare, but it was what the base wanted to hear. He also knew that he couldn't prevent these large corporations from leaving this country in order to stay competitive, but he said what the blue-collar red states wanted to hear. He knew that if these events didn't take place, all he had to do was blame the Democrats and people would believe him even though the Republicans controlled all three branches of government. A large segment of the country are not readers and depend on others to tell them what they should do and think. "I am not," as Hillary said, "calling them deplorable, just uninformed."

What President Trump does is create a smoke screen of another issue, as he did with the NFL kneeling protests, to take our focus off his failed attempts at repealing the Affordable Care Act as well as the investigations of his alleged ties to Russia. What he accomplished in that particular kneeling scenario was to take the focus off the fact of the inhumane police brutality against black and brown people and place it on disrespect of the flag and the military. Can you see what he did? He fed red meat to his base as well as to the people who wore the American flag on their backs but with hate in their hearts.

There was a time when the presidency was well respected no matter who was in the Oval Office. Now lying, self-interest, misogyny, showmanship, incompetence, and tyranny are indicative of this administration and its lack of soul. I know it seems that I am excessively rough on this president, but like others, you have to earn the respect. It can't be legislated. Earlier, I defined *soul* as "the essence or embodiment of a specific quality or the spiritual or immaterial part of a human being or animal regarded as immortal." This president has proven, time and time again, that he has no soul and no moral compass, and that is a dangerous combination.

Since the current administration invaded and infested the White House, they have, as with other administrations, taken credit for what the prior administration started–the good trends, that is. Just recently, our president–who self-proclaims himself to be smarter than the generals, less racist than anyone, and best educated–is now attempting to take credit for black unemployment being at its lowest level ever. The economic recovery had already started under President Obama, and black unemployment is following the same pattern.

Draw a line across either unemployment or the economy, and you will see that the recovery was in high gear before this president ever set foot in the Oval Office. He is right that the unemployment numbers for blacks (6.8 percent) and Hispanics (4.9 percent) are lowest since the government started to track the numbers back in

1972, but he is taking credit for these lower rates when, in fact, these rates have been falling since 2010, which was the beginning of the Obama years.

According to the "real numbers" that are not "fake news," it doesn't look like the change has been that significant. The truth be told, the average job creation in the first year of the Trump administration is slightly lower than it has been in prior years. Employers added 171,000 new jobs each month on average in 2017; in 2016, the average was 187,000; and in 2015, it was 226,000. So you can make these claims as long as no one fact-checks the data.

Momentum, not the "genius" or any "art of the deal" of Trump, is responsible for these improving numbers. It's shameful to point out that black people are doing "better than ever before" when the numbers are still high. The white unemployment rate is at approximately 3.5 percent, and the culture is 78 percent of the total population. Realistically, these numbers pale to where other cultures are, including those cultures who entered the country much later than blacks. Even Latino and Asian unemployment rates are better than African Americans. This president thinks that more money in the pocket is the focal point when blacks are being disrespected and marginalized on a daily basis.

This so-called president doesn't even realize that his demonstrated low expectations for people of color are signs of his racist demeanor. His "shit–– counties" comment, his treatment of the people of Puerto Rico after the hurricane, his comments about the demonstrations in Charlottesville, his treatment of Gold Star families, and his comments to Billy Bush on the bus ride about women are all indicators of who this man truly is.

The late Maya Angelou wrote, "When someone shows you who they are, believe them the first time." It took the White House twenty-two days to acknowledge Waffle House hero James Shaw, who stopped a shooter unarmed and then raised $250,000 for the victims. In retrospect, it took Trump twenty-four hours, according to news reports, to acknowledge white supremacist Tomi Lahren for getting a drink thrown at her. Now I ask you, Is this president consciously biased?

It's all over the "fake news," as Trump calls it, that he is ecstatic to cite the unemployment rate for African Americans, bragging that it's the best in the history of the country.

The jobless rate for African Americans had already fallen under the Obama administration when Trump took the oath of office, so Trump taking credit for this is like him taking credit for having a larger crowd at his inauguration than Barack Obama. Even Ray Charles and Stevie Wonder could see that he was, once again, living in his own fantasy world. The one thing that is painfully clear is that he is an apprentice in the most powerful position in the world. I would be ecstatic to hear the words, "Benedict Donald, you are fired."

CHAPTER 8

The Color Divide

It's never too late to give up your prejudice.
—Henry David Thoreau

IN THE PAST election, the white evangelicals and the Christian right voted in overwhelming numbers for Donald Trump. On the surface, that is their right, but I advise them to change their message from the pulpit. Preaching love thy neighbor, family values, purity, and repentance is not in line with the total support that was given by these church leaders to someone like Trump, who is in constant violation of those principles. In golfing terms, they were too willing to give him a mulligan. A mulligan is a second chance to perform an action, usually after the first chance went wrong through bad luck or a blunder. How many chances does one person get, and would they have given Obama the same opportunity if he had committed the atrocities that Trump has? The answer is a resounding "Absolutely not."

They gave him a mulligan in his discussion with Billy Bush where he disrespected women during their bus ride. They said it was simply locker-room talk. They gave him another mulligan when he refused to reveal his taxes as all other presidents have done. They gave him a mulligan on his alleged relationships to porn star Stormy Daniels and *Playboy* model Karen McDougal. They gave him a mulligan for the 132 times he has played golf since becoming president at a cost to the taxpayer of tens of millions of dollars. In comparison, President Obama played golf 306 times in eight years. If you remember, President Trump was critical of President Obama for playing golf as much as he did. He was given a mulligan for refusing to attend military and international briefings with the Defense Department. Mr. President, your mulligans are running out.

The evangelicals actually cheered the outcome, reassuring uneasy fellow worshippers with talk of abortion and religious liberty, about how politics is the art of compromise rather than the ideal. Why is the Christian right so strongly in the Trump camp? As long as any GOP presidential candidates promise to advance at least the antiabortion and religious liberty agendas by appointing conservative judges, they gain and keep Christian right support. The other agendas that captivate and secure these voters are partisanship, antigay, antiabortion, and antifeminist.

Christians of color entered the political fray because of Trump's open hostility toward black NFL players protesting police brutality as well as his earlier "birther" crusade against President Obama. Trump's false claims of Obama not being a United States citizen galvanized the black community and made us realize that these negatives on the part of this individual were a signal of things to come.

From 2014 to 2017, there had been an exodus of black worshippers to white megachurch establishments. This change of attitude toward a more mega establishment came as a result of a lack of infrastructure, financial improprieties, failed relationships among members, and pastoral leadership disappointments. Initially, they found the mixed, more organized, and financially independent megachurches to be a breath of fresh air.

In these megachurches, they were smiling greeters welcoming everyone to the services, with plenty of parking space, free pastries and coffee, shopping areas, ATM machines, children changing areas, childcare while you attended services, etc. Then there was a new president replacing one who, even without governmental support, was basically loved by the people. He was one who never had any noise around his family, his image, or his ability to run the most powerful nation in the world. He was a president who took his responsibilities seriously and placed the country before his political aspirations.

Now consider what we have in our current president, Trump. He is one who is a megabusinessman, a philanderer, a liar, and obviously a racist based on his attacks mainly on people of color. He shows a lack of leadership and refuses to take on the NRA and gun control in the face of continued school shootings and weapons of mass destruction made available to those who are not successfully screened.

What does this have to do with the subject, you may ask. Well, those blacks and other minorities who were a part of the exodus to these megachurches are finding themselves isolated in an environment that doesn't share their ideas, their values, or their interests. The pastors of these megachurches, though pleasant and engaging, refuse to address the issues pertinent to these new entrants. They refuse to deal with rogue police gunning down black and brown people in the streets. They even fail to criticize President Trump on issues that go against their religious ideologies. They are more than willing to give him a mulligan on many of his misssteps because their feelings of homogeneity with him remain strong where similar feelings were not as strong for a black president who didn't come from their world. They cheered the outcome, reassuring uneasy fellow worshippers with talks of abortion and religious liberty, about how politics is the art of compromise rather than the ideal.

Christians of color, even those who shared these policy preferences, looked at Mr. Trump's comments about Mexican immigrants, his open hostility toward

NFL players protesting police brutality, and his earlier "birther" crusade against President Obama, claiming falsely he was not a United States citizen, as opening a wound that even religion and theology cannot heal.

These diverse parishioners are feeling disenfranchised and unsure of their future. They want to leave but are confused by whether to rejoin past congregations that had failed them in the first place or sit at home and listen to Joel Osteen. My research says that many are choosing to stay home and engage in television ministries. Many of these parishioners fall completely away from the church, and their religious beliefs tend to dissipate because in their minds, there are few alternatives and the system had failed them.

It is true that more established ministers like T. D. Jakes, Eddie Long (deceased), Creflo Dollar, Charles Blake Sr., and many others are a part of a trend toward megachurches in the black community. Many African American preachers look toward these churches as models of where they wish to be and attempt to immolate them by placing unreasonable demands on their memberships.

One such request on the part of these megachurches is requiring members to submit their W-2 forms to ensure that they are donating their 10 percent as suggested in the Old Testament. But is a megachurch a good model of good spiritual hygiene? It's between me and God whether I am obligated to pay 10 percent of my earnings to the church. Is the 10 percent all in monetary funds or do the 10 percent include personal time given in service to the church? It's a debate that will rage on in the minds of those who interpret the testament in a multitude of ways.

Dr. Shayna Lee stated, "We have approached a new era in American Protestantism where neo-Pentecostal megachurches represent the greatest challenge that the traditional black church has ever faced."

These megachurches, often nondenominational, have reduced the resources available in many of the more traditional smaller black churches that are connected often to denominations. They have often set up their own denominational-like structures where they publish their own materials, have their own camp meetings, etc. Sometimes these megachurches have little to no accountability for their leaders. They are accountable to no one. Such a situation can cause abuse and corruption if the infrastructure and accountability are lacking.

Even in the black churches where there is an infrastructure of deacons, trustees and finance committees, usher boards, etc., problems still exist because of lack of accountability on the part of the heads of these suborganizations. As in society, these church organizations fail to hold its leaders accountable based on bylaws and financial regulations. The minister, pastor, or evangelist who is the appointed head of the church tends to develop his or her own set of dutiful followers who are willing to bend the rules to keep the head of the organization happy. Conversely, the head or pastor develops a belief that the church belongs to him or her and that rules no longer apply as it relates to these set of laws and regulations. If the head is corrupt, the body tends to struggle or die. Many churches start out applying the rules as they are intended. After a sustained period of growth and prosperity, many tend to go off the rails because of financial improprieties and lack of leadership. The signs of such a decaying structure are the following:

- ✓ A lack of young people participating in the church.
- ✓ Choir participation has dwindled.
- ✓ Decrease in the tithing of its members.
- ✓ Individuals with the skill sets are unwilling to serve in key roles.
- ✓ Violations to church bylaws.
- ✓ Lack of trust between the pastor and his leadership team.
- ✓ Lack of young people attending the establishment.

Why did the evangelical right feel so strongly about supporting President Trump when they were all but nonexistent in the campaign of Barrack Obama? Leading up to Election Day, the buzz surrounding candidate Trump included a heavy dose of confusion. Trump, like many GOP candidates, not only worked to court evangelicals but also repeatedly flubbed attempts to talk coherently about religion throughout his campaign. He has been unable to name his favorite book of the Bible. He said that he doesn't ask for forgiveness from God because he's "not making mistakes," appeared confused about the beliefs of the Presbyterian denomination he claims, and evoked laughter while speaking at Liberty University by referring to a book of the Bible as "Two

Corinthians" instead of the more common phrase "Second Corinthians."

So why do men and women of God throw their reputations and respective religions under the bus to support this president? How could these evangelicals, a group known for their pursuit of spiritual purity and fairness, support a twice-divorced, theologically challenged, discriminating, misogynistic man like Donald Trump? It makes one question just how faith-based many of these religious leaders really are. We must remember that they are men and women just like us and are capable of the brainwashing as the rest of us are, especially as it relates to their political beliefs.

Let's dissect what the president really meant about his election theme–"Let's Make America Great Again" or was it a dog whistle for "Let's go back to a time when the white majority was unquestionably in total control of everything, a time when the majority of Mexicans and Latino cultures were predominately in Latin America and Spain." Prospecting for gold in California brought many Chinese to America. They took jobs as laborers in places like Hawaii, where they worked on sugarcane plantations and in other parts of the Western United States. While in places like California, Chinese miners experienced their first taste of discrimination in the form of the foreign miners' tax. This was supposed to be collected from every foreign miner, but in reality, it was only collected from the Chinese, despite the multitude of miners from European countries.

These facts ring loud and clear to those who value the culture enough to become a student of the data. Many of these behaviors and actions were duplications of the slavery experience. Each culture of color has taken their seats at the table of oppression and degradation written on the crowns of our heads by those who chose to benefit from our blood, sweat, and tears. As long as our services benefit the powerful, we were relatively safe though oppressed. However, the white gold miners began to resent the Chinese miners, feeling that they were discovering gold that the white miners deserved.

In 1852, a special foreign miners' tax aimed at the Chinese was passed by the California legislature. This tax required a payment of three dollars each month at a time when Chinese miners were making approximately six dollars a month. Tax collectors could legally take and sell the property of those miners who refused or could not pay the tax. Fake tax collectors made money by taking advantage of people who couldn't speak English well, and some tax collectors, both false and real, stabbed or shot miners who couldn't or wouldn't pay the tax.

The Trump administration, and specifically President Trump himself, categorized people from primarily Mexico as murderers and rapists. Was he speaking of a time when there were fewer of the Spanish-speaking cultures in the country? How did the Spanish culture fair in early America? In the United States, before there was New England, there was New Spain; and before there was Boston, Massachusetts, there was Santa Fe, New Mexico.

The teaching of American history normally emphasizes the founding and growth of the British colonies in North America, their emergence as an independent nation in 1776, and the development of the United States from east to west. This treatment easily omits the fact that there was significant colonization by Spain of what is now the American Southwest. It also tends to ignore, until the Mexican War is mentioned, that the whole Southwest, from Texas westward to California, was a Spanish-speaking territory with its own distinctive heritage, culture, and customs for many decades.

The Spanish-speaking citizens of the United States who were incorporated into the country as a result of the Mexican War are called Mexican Americans. Their numbers have since increased as a result of immigration. Other Spanish-speaking citizens came from Cuba and Puerto Rico, and smaller numbers are immigrants from Central and South America and from the Dominican Republic. Taken together, these people are called Hispanics or Latinos. Hispanics today form the fastest-growing ethnic minority in the United States. Numbering about 22.4 million in 1992, they make up the second-largest minority in the nation, African Americans being the largest. About 60 percent of these Hispanics trace their origin to Mexico. Although Hispanics have experienced less outright discrimination (except in Texas and New Mexico) than have African Americans, some sections of this group have lower economic and education levels than the rest of the population in the United States.

Puerto Ricans enjoy a different status from other Hispanics in that they are citizens of the United States by birth, whether they were born in their homeland or in the United States. They were granted citizenship in 1917. (Puerto Rico became a possession of the United States as a result of the Spanish-American War.) They may therefore go back and forth between the island and the mainland without visas or passports. Mexicans, Cubans, and others must enter the country as immigrants with alien status and must apply for citizenship in the same way as do other immigrants.

Although there are Hispanics in most parts of the United States, some areas have especially large concentrations. Eighty-six (86) percent of Mexican Americans make their homes in five Southwestern states: Texas, California, New Mexico, Arizona, and Colorado. There are two basic reasons for Hispanic immigration to the United States: economic opportunity and escape from political persecution. Very large numbers of Mexicans and Puerto Ricans entered the country to escape poverty and to find a way to make a living. The twentieth-century Cuban migration, which began in 1959 when Fidel Castro took over the government of Cuba, was mainly for political reasons. (Data was sourced from various unknown authors.)

Now we know how we blacks came to America, but white America sometimes turn a blind eye to their role in the immigration boom. Slavery was a stain on America's past that cannot be removed by ignoring history or by refusing to include much of it in school textbooks. Many high schools and colleges/universities actually refuse to carry black studies courses. African Americans (also referred to as black Americans or Afro-Americans) are an ethnic group of Americans with total or partial ancestry from any of the black racial groups of Africa. The term typically refers to descendants of enslaved black people who were from the United States. As a compound adjective, the term is usually hyphenated as *African-American*. Black and African Americans constitute the third-largest racial and ethnic group in the United States (after white Americans and Hispanic and Latino Americans). Most African Americans are descendants of enslaved peoples within the boundaries of the present United States.

Could this be the times that Old Donald was referring to? Or maybe it was what happened to the American Indian. Let's visit some of this history. Native Americans—also known as American Indians, Indians, indigenous Americans, and other terms—are the indigenous (originating in and characteristic of a particular region or country) peoples of the United States. There are over five hundred federally recognized tribes within the US, about half of which are associated with Indian reservations. The term excludes Native Hawaiians and some Alaska Natives. The ancestors of modern Native Americans arrived in what is now the United States at least fifteen thousand years ago, possibly much earlier, from Asia via Beringia. A vast variety of peoples, societies, and cultures subsequently developed. Native Americans were greatly affected by the European colonization of the Americas, which began in 1492, and their population declined precipitously due to introduced diseases, warfare, and slavery.

After the founding of the United States, many Native American peoples were subjected to warfare, removals, and one-sided treaties, and they continued to suffer from discriminatory government policies today. Since the 1960s, Native American self-determination movements have resulted in many changes to the lives of Native Americans, though there are still many contemporary issues faced by Native Americans. Today, there are over five million Native Americans in the United States (Wikipedia).

Could any of these periods be the dog whistle of a time in the small mind of this president as a time he would love to see return? Calling Klansmen and neo-Nazis good people while not commenting on domestic terrorist as he does for those coming from Islamic cultures, are these signs of a deeper racist tone that this president has placed on the world stage? Is it the fact that he has openly attacked Gold Star families because of the color of their skin or even the attack on John McCain, senator from Arizona, who refused to bow and kiss his ring?

Is it the beginning of fascism, a form of radical authoritarian ultranationalism characterized by dictatorial power, forcible suppression of opposition, and control of industry and commerce, which came to prominence in early twentieth-century Europe? This president is the most power-hungry, self-absorbed, self-declared pundit. The most dangerous part of this is that he believes his own lies. Any person who can lie as easily as this president cannot be trusted with the nuclear codes. Any president who so easily attacks his own defense department, the intelligence community, and free press is a danger to himself as well as the country. He is a self-proclaimed pundit, and he knows more about the military than the generals of this country. If he is indeed a pundit and expert as he claims, how often do his GOP colleagues call on him to give his opinion to the general public? I rest my case.

What is it? Is it calling the news media fake for being transparent on his improprieties, accusing his own FBI of bias against him, refusing to criticize Russia and Putin for violating our sovereignty, reversing all the good things that the prior administration did, and attacking his own justice department under the leadership of Jeff Sessions, whom he appointed? Or could it be that we, the voters, who either put him in the job or those of us who failed to elect Hillary Clinton, are truly to blame for what organized chaos we are experiencing from this White House?

Why does Trump's political base still love him in spite of his antics? Trump won most men, most white millennials, about half of wealthy Americans, most college-educated white voters, and most independents. But this is uncommon in Hollywood when portraying Trump supporters. Exit polls from the 2016 election showed that the majority of voters, without college degrees, backed Trump. Lacking a college degree is not always the same as being on the working class.

American National Election Studies reports that nearly 60 percent of white Trump supporters without college degrees were in the top half of the income distribution. In fact, one in five white Trump voters without a college degree lives in households where the income exceeds $100,000. But exit polling did not include how people earned a living. President Donald Trump is an entertainer, and he knows how to play a crowd. He plays to the fears and needs of his base. He promises to build a wall to protect American workers from the scourge of immigrants taking their jobs and raping their wives and daughters. Trump promises to bring back coal jobs, which he knows is virtually impossible, and promises to penalize companies who refuse to bring jobs and large amounts of offshore funds back into the United States. He is a bait-and-switch artist who confuses weak-minded people with his ability to take the attention off one issue by creating another. He has been able to do that with his base as related to the issues about Russia, his finances, the Trump Tower meeting, who is paying for the wall, etc.

It is my belief that the "Make America Great Again" slogan refers to a period when people of color had their "place," a time when private golf clubs were a tradition; when cotton fields were filled with black workers; when blacks and other people of color only succeeded in sports and entertainment; when sports like auto racing, swimming, polo, tennis, and baseball and owning a business, becoming president, owning a nice home, and being a millionaire were reserved primarily for those in the majority. I do believe this to be his vision. I have news for you, Mr. Trump. You will never see those days again, no matter how much you and your base would love to revisit them.

Immigration will continue to be the backbone and foundation of this country in medicine, research, construction, agriculture, sports, and entertainment whether you like it or not, Mr. President. Your desire to be Putin will never be realized; your disrespect for women will be the obstacle around the curve that will not play well for you. Your desire to be a dictator or oligarch will only be realized in some other countries, so I hope your bromance with Putin results in a marriage–in Russia. America, I say again, have we lost our soul?

This president speaks often about draining the swamp, but he continues to surround himself with shady characters like Steve Bannon. Bannon was once vice president of the firm that specialized in the collection of data and the creation of strategies to change public behavior.

Bannon sees cultural warfare as the means to create enduring change in American politics according to Christopher Wylie, identified as a whistleblower. "It was for this reason Mr. Bannon engaged SCL, a foreign military contractor, to build an arsenal of informational weapons he could deploy on the American population." Bannon was once vice president of the firm of an offshoot of British company SCL, which specialized in the collection of data and the creation of strategies to change public behavior. Cambridge Analytica announced its closure following damaging allegations about misuse of social media data, and one of the men behind the accusations said promoting conflict was Bannon's goal in using the company's resources.

What manner of man is this, and why does Trump feel a kinship with such a dark figure? This man is a follower of something called the Breitbart doctrine, which assumes that politics is downstream from culture. He believes that if you want any lasting or enduring changes in politics, you have to focus on the culture," Wylie added, according to CBS News. (When Steve Bannon used the term *culture war*, he used that term pointedly, and they were seeking out companies that could build an arsenal of informational weapons to fight that war.) Is employing this man Bannon as the right hand to the president draining the swamp? Is he draining the swamp or adding another wing to it?

This won't be the last of "draining the swamp." Once people find the light switch in the White House, they are getting out of the dark. Expect to see more of the same based on the erratic nature of the presidency—ones that immediately come to mind are Kellyanne Conway, counsel to the president; Jeff Sessions, attorney general; John Kelly, chief of staff; and maybe even Trump himself. I ask again, has America lost its soul? A radical element of law enforcement is unjustly gunning down primarily black and brown men and women in the streets for minor violations and using the "I feared for my life" defense to justify their actions, a "stand your ground" law in some states that allow citizens to gun down other citizens because of the fear factor. Most white individuals who commit crime will most often live unless they decide to end their own lives. This is not the same with black and brown citizens–it's "shoot first and shoot to kill because our lives are not valued on equal grounds with those in the majority culture."

A defense of "I thought he had a weapon" or "I felt my life was being threatened" seems to be the get-out-of-jail card for many of those sworn to protect and serve us. Why are their segments of the body camera's tape missing? Why are some cameras not activated? If these police officers and women are held accountable for their actions and our justice system sends a strong message to these violators of true justice, we can heal the wounds of bias that has obviously separated us. What if it was one of their relatives at the other end of the gun? That never crosses their minds because the chances of that happening are very remote at best.

We tend to judge a person's character by those we surround ourselves with and how we behave as a result of those relationships.

CHAPTER 9

Kneeling Has Its Purpose

If you defend free speech for bigots but not to combat bigotry, then you believe in bigotry, not free speech.
—DaShanne Stokes

THE ISSUE OF kneeling during the national anthem has placed on the front pages of our national news whether there is a right to free expression guaranteed by the First Amendment or not. When the president of the United States decided that this issue was more important than North Korea, Russia meddling in our democracy, immigration rights, nuclear proliferation, criminal justice reform, and international leadership, it gave us a peek at his comfort with issues that can divide the country. These are evidences that his lack of preparedness to understand and grasp the real and tangible issues facing us as US citizens makes him unfit for this lofty office.

He is so obsessed with his popularity, crowd size at his rallies, and in addressing issues counter to the needs of a diverse society. This president involved himself in a football player kneeling during the national anthem. Was it because he has yet to grasp the specifics of real-world issues and his responsibilities as commander-in-chief? His main focus is not the needs of the country but, instead, his desire to play to and fire up his base and those who feel that kneeling during the national anthem is disrespectful to the military and to the country.

I have a different perspective. I am a black man who served in the military, and the kneeling didn't bother me at all. The First Amendment to the United States Constitution prevents Congress from making any law respecting an establishment of religion, prohibiting the free exercise of religion, or abridging the freedom of speech, the freedom of the press, and the right to peaceably assemble or to petition for a governmental redress of grievances. It was adopted on December 15, 1791, as one of the ten amendments that constitute the Bill of Rights.

Below is a summary of what the First Amendment includes. Some may decide to interpret it in a way that supports their ideas or their way of life, but I, too, fought for these freedoms that the president has decided to try and take away. You don't want to regulate guns and you want to play bait and switch with the flag issue, but the right to free speech has to be protected, and Trump or no other source should have the power to redact it. These rights are clearly stated, and the First Amendment states, in relevant part, that "Congress shall make no law . . . abridging freedom of speech."

Freedom of speech includes the right

- ➢ not to speak (specifically, the right not to salute the flag),
- ➢ of students to wear black armbands to school to protest a war,
- ➢ to use certain offensive words and phrases to convey political messages,
- ➢ to contribute money (under certain circumstances) to political campaigns,
- ➢ to advertise commercial products and professional services (with some restrictions), and
- ➢ to engage in symbolic speech (e.g., burning the flag in protest).

Freedom of speech does not include the right

- ➢ to incite actions that would harm others,
- ➢ to make or distribute obscene materials,
- ➢ to burn draft cards as an antiwar protest,
- ➢ to permit students to print articles in a school newspaper over the objections of the school administration,
- ➢ of students to make an obscene speech at a school-sponsored event, and
- ➢ of students to advocate illegal drug use at a school-sponsored event.

Freedom of speech is simply the right of people to express their opinions publicly without governmental interference, subject to the laws against libel, incitement to violence or rebellion, etc. Now is that plan enough for you? Mr. Trump, stay out of sports and try your best to learn how to represent all the people all the time, which is something that has been elusive in your behavior.

I served in Vietnam and respect the anthem and flag, but I do understand that the anthem did not have my people in mind when it was written. It spoke about the death of slaves who fought for the British against the Americans. For owners to tell players that they had to stand for the anthem, as Jimmy Jones of the Dallas Cowboys did, reeks of 2017 apartheid. I have a right to kneel just as you have the right to stand. This great country, which we are a part of, has given us that right through the First Amendment.

Demographics are important here. According to a report from the Institute for Diversity and Ethics in Sport (TIDES), the NFL's players are nearly 70 percent black. In sharp contrast, quarterbacks are only 19 percent black. Head coaches are only 21.9 percent black. There is not a single black owner of a team. According to the Sentencing Project, one in three black men born in 2001 will end up in prison at some point in their lives—compared to one in seventeen white men. Black men are more likely to be arrested, be convicted, and serve longer prison terms than other cultures. Of those in prison, one in nine is serving a life sentence—with about a third not eligible for parole. Overall, people of color make up 67 percent of the incarcerated population but just 37 percent of the population overall. The disparities are hard to ignore, but apparently not for Trump and the NFL owners.

The NFL demonstration, on the part of the players, was a peaceful demonstration of their First Amendment rights as stated above. It was made clear, so we thought in the beginning, it was not an attempt to disrespect the military or the flag, and Trump knew it. It was his way of taking the focus off the police who are killing unarmed brown and black women and men all over the country in alarming numbers. He knew that the anthem is a sensitive subject and he could rile the base, and he did. This was the typical bait-and-switch tactic, which has become a trademark of the Trump administration. We all remember when Trump said, "You know what else they say about my people? The polls, they say I have the most loyal people. Did you ever see that, where I could stand in the middle of Fifth Avenue and shoot somebody and I wouldn't lose any voters, okay? It's like incredible."

He was right. Those who are in his camp can't see how this man will say anything at the moment. He promised that he would bring jobs back to this country and it would be easy. Well, one and a half years into his presidency, jobs are still leaving because these large corporations will focus on what is best for their bottom line. Cheap labor and lower cost of production will continue to drive jobs to other countries. He went on to lie to the hardworking people in the coal industry. Coal is dead as a major source fossil fuel and has been tremendously damaging to the environment. The primary reason that fossil fuels are harmful to the environment is that they produce large amounts of greenhouse gases. These gases cause heat to build up in the atmosphere and raise the average temperature of the planet.

Fossil fuels also pollute the air when they're burned and may cause environmental damage when they're mined. This man knew when he made the promise that wind, natural gas, and solar are the energy sources of the future, but he fed the base in coal country what they wanted to hear to get the nomination. That same voting base turned on Hillary for telling the truth. She damaged her credibility with her base when she rolled back some of the comments instead of sticking with her guns.

What happened to the wall that Mexico was surely going to pay for? Now if there is ever a wall, you can bet your paycheck that the American taxpayer will foot the bill. Anyone who can lie with a straight face, like this president, is a dangerous politician. The attacks on Syria were simply a political ploy where both Russia and Syria knew exactly what was to happen prior to the attacks. It allowed Trump to temporarily ease the pressure of his failed presidency back home. Neither attack did anything to limit Syria's capability to launch their air strikes or deliver lethal nerve gas to its own people.

The Donald promised during the campaign to "lock her up" in reference to Hillary Clinton and the email fiasco. What has happened since? Absolutely *nothing*! He claimed to have proof that past president Barrack Obama was not a citizen of the United States—wrong again. Another large nothing burger. Then there was the North American Free Trade Agreement that is still hanging by a thread. The total repeal of Obamacare would leave millions of Americans without health insurance. At the moment, Obamacare will be available everywhere unless repealed. At times it seemed as if tens of thousands of Americans might not have any options on their Obamacare exchanges as insurers fled the market amid the uncertainty emanating from Washington, DC. But other carriers eventually stepped in to make sure coverage was maintained.

Trump was proud of himself for convincing his base to believe that canceling the Iran deal was a big win. We will see. He wanted to bomb and take the oil fields from ISIS. Not going to happen, Mr. President. Folks, these empty promises go on and on, and yes, he is given unyielding support from his base who stands in the crosshairs of his ineptness.

With issues like North Korea, tax reform, disasters, Russia's interference in our free election process, voter suppression, and internal conflict within the administration, there should be no patience with his bait-and-switch tactics. His GOP constituents are so afraid that he will personally attack them if they run for another term in future elections they fade into the background even though they know he is wrong. Trump knew that feeding red meat to the sharks would cause all the carnivorous hate mongrels to flap their fins.

Charlie Sykes, political commentator, said it best when he stated, "We all live in Trump's crab bucket. If you can't win respect, then you try to destroy the basis by which respect is granted by flattening the moral landscape. Because President Trump is incapable of appreciating or emulating Senator John McCain's sense of duty and honor [Trump dodged the draft], he resorts to the petulance of the bitter and envious. Many of this administration's actions have been predicated on the reverse of the gains of the country under President Obama.

This president, with his smug and racist attitude, has refused to apologize even when it's obvious that wrong was done as in the case of the two black men who were arrested simply for "sitting and relaxing while black." They had met at a Philadelphia Starbucks to discuss real estate and were charged by one of its employees of trespassing. Starbucks CEO, Kevin Johnson, met with the two young men to apologize for the way they had been treated by both the manager and the police. I, on many occasions, have gone into Starbucks and have observed many whites who are simply relaxing, using the computer, or simply reading the newspaper. I don't ever recall anyone calling the cops on them.

There was another case where the president of Nordstrom Rack, Geevy Thomas flew down to Saint Louis, Missouri, to offer a face-to-face apology to three black teens who were wrongly accused by store employees of shoplifting. The controversy began after Mekhi Lee, Dirone Taylor, and Eric Rogers II said they noticed several store employees following them around the Nordstrom Rack Brentwood Square, where they were shopping for prom clothes. Although the teens made purchases, they were stopped outside the store by several Brentwood police officers who told them the store employees had accused them of theft. "We did not handle this situation well, and we apologized to these young men and their families," a company spokesperson said in a statement. "We want all customers to feel welcome when they shop with us, and we do not tolerate discrimination of any kind." Just another case of "shopping while black." Again, I wonder how often this happened to those of the majority race.

Shall I continue? There was the case of the black women who were playing too slow at the golf course when one of the course employees called the police. Now is this good use of our police who are paid to protect and serve? Who were they protecting? Had there been a crime committed? This is a case of harassment and bigotry by the golf course white members for the women "putting while black." If law enforcement begins to charge these bigots with misuse of federal and state resources, this crap will stop.

Lolade Siyonbola, a graduate student in African studies at Yale, fell asleep while working on a "marathon of papers" Monday night. On Tuesday, a white woman who lived in the dorm turned on the lights and called the Yale police, telling Ms. Siyonbola she wasn't allowed to sleep there. Several officers arrived, and Ms. Siyonbola showed them the key to her apartment and her ID. Though the officers were not at fault for following procedure, the incident should have never happened. Kimberly M. Goff-Crews, the university's vice president for student life, said in an email to students that she was "deeply troubled" by the episode. On Thursday, Yale made a point to emphasize that officers had told the caller that this was not a police matter—if that student was white! You know the rest. Yet another case of the police being called on a person who was "napping while black."

I couldn't make this stuff up. There was the case of the three black people loading suitcases into their car after staying at an Airbnb in Rialto, California, on April 30, but they were halted by the police after a neighbor suspected they were burglars. A white neighbor felt the need to call the police because the individuals did not wave to her. It was simply because these black folks didn't fit the landscape. They were questioned by officers as a helicopter flew overhead. Airbnb said in a statement that the guests' treatment was "unconscionable." Is this a case of "vacationing while black"? Then there was a former Obama White House staff member who was moving into a new apartment. Again, a white caller didn't think he fit the landscape and called the police. This was a case of "renting while black."

This has all happened in the first year of this racist administration. Another similar case was uncovered when a black family was simply enjoying a barbecue at the lake when the police were called because they didn't fit the landscape—yet another case of "barbequing while black." Finally, there was the case of a black real estate investor who was inspecting one of his properties that he refurbished and resold. A white neighbor called the police, and even the police felt that her actions were outlandish and bordered on the ridiculous—again, a case of "investing while black." This is indicative of a lot of reserved hatred resulting from eight years of having a black man in the White House. This is racial profiling at the highest level, which has been emboldened by the actions and rhetoric of this "New Trump America."

Just to show the difference in his racist beliefs, a white Fox News employee had a cup of water thrown on her because of her conservative racist views on her show. Within hours, Trump had villainized those responsible when it was twenty-two days before he commented on the young black man who stopped a domestic terrorist from killing more people in a Waffle House in Alabama. It took him –– days to comment on the Santa Fe High School in Texas. Sad!

What is the genesis of these incidents? Why does this administration turn a blind eye and deaf ear to these incidents? We know why. Prior administrations had similar events take place but reacted differently. People with these pent-up racist views feel comfortable releasing their frustrations under the new administration, who shouts, "Lock them up!" "Knock the hell out of the son of a bitch!" "Fake news!" and "Witch hunt!"

He takes credit for the low unemployment rate for blacks in many of his campaign-like speeches to his base. He is right that black unemployment hit an all-time low in December 2017, not only falling to its lowest level since the Great Recession but falling below 7 percent for the first time since the statistic began being recorded. Given that black unemployment hit a high point of around 16.7 percent in August 2011 as the country recovered from the Great Recession, the new number is ostensibly good news. But exactly how much progress the new 6.8 percent number reflects and what role Trump played in getting it there aren't exactly what the president says. There is still nothing to celebrate in these numbers.

Fact-checkers have noted that the Donald has had basically a minor contribution to the decline. Unemployment among black Americans has been declining pretty steadily after coming close to 17 percent in 2011. Philip Bump of the *Washington Post* points out that unemployment numbers for black Americans have fallen relatively consistent for the past several years. By the time Trump entered the Oval Office in January 2017, the black unemployment rate was at 7.8 percent.

"From January to December 2017, the unemployment rate among black Americans fell 1 percentage point," Bump explains. "During the same period in 2016, it fell the same amount. In 2015, it fell 1.9 points. The previous year, it fell 1.5 points. The year before that, it fell 1.8 points." Jared Bernstein, a senior fellow at the Center on Budget and Policy Priorities and a former economic adviser to Vice President Joe Biden, says Trump can't really take credit for this trajectory. "Trump has had nothing to do with the decline in African American jobless rates or any other group's rates," Bernstein told Vox. "He's completely riding a trend he inherited." Instead, Bernstein credits the actions of Federal Reserve chair Janet Yellen, who oversaw a steady period of declining unemployment numbers and kept interest rates suppressed instead of raising them as soon as the unemployment numbers fell, a move that helped drive unemployment down further. Yellen was frequently criticized by the GOP and then candidate Trump, who argued on the campaign trail that the unemployment rate was a "phony number."

He challenges the experts, and his base sticks with him though they know he is wrong because his beliefs are their beliefs, his lies are their lies, and his failures are their failures. They totally identify with a man who doesn't know the difference between HIV (human immunodeficiency virus) and HPV (human papillomavirus). He does not have the confidence in himself to hold open press conferences and doesn't have the patience to review detailed military reports. He is more comfortable on the golf course than in the Oval Office. Mr. Trump was indeed unprepared to take the seat in the highest office in the land and fill its shoes.

Many of the above comments and facts are the real symptoms of what a danger this administration is to all of us. Their own self-absorption and lack of real concern for Middle America will thrust us into a downward spiral that can and will undo the gains and prosperity of the middle class for decades to come. If we buy into the rhetoric of these oligarchs, middle class as we know it will all but disappear. We would move more into a realm of the "haves and the have-nots." If they take away our right to kneel at a sports event, what else will they take away? Prayer in schools and the Ten Commandments have already been taken away as the foundation of what we all grew up believing and respecting. What's next?

Has America lost its soul? We tend to have more respect for gun rights, the life of animals, and wealth than we have for human rights and specifically the rights of certain cultures. Sad!

CHAPTER 10

Obama Fixation

You become what you think about all day long.
—Ralph Waldo Emerson

WHY IS PRESIDENT Trump so obsessed with negating everything that Obama touched while in office? I am glad you asked. It is simply because Obama is more talented, smarter, more presidential, articulate (there is that word), qualified, charismatic, mature, popular, respected by most, and classy. Here are the signs that he is just a jealous, rich, minimal-vocabulary, hateful, racist, and vindictive man. He rode to victory on Russia's help, ill-advised Comey statements about emails, a country fearful of a woman presidency, and Hillary's failure to seize the moment in key battleground states by not campaigning in the latter stages of the campaign. Hillary is living proof that complacency can cost you the top prize. The media, the polls, everybody, including Trump, thought that this was a cakewalk for her, but politics, Russia, WikiLeaks, missed opportunity, and overconfidence had turned a Cinderella story into a nightmare.

Some of the most ridiculous actions that Trump had undertaken was to reverse the pardon of the turkeys that Obama had pardoned during Thanksgiving. He supported every attempt to repeal and replace Obamacare (for those of you who didn't know, it's also called the Affordable Care Act), and to no surprise, his justice department under the guidance, or the lack thereof, of Attorney General Jeff Sessions is in the process of undoing all the gains that minority, women, transgender, and LGBTQ individuals made under the Obama administration.

America's slavery was directly tied to what many of the current administration believe to be "when America was great" and white dominance as was stated by Judge Roy Moore during his campaign to represent Alabama in the US Senate. I totally agree with Annette Gordon-Reed when she said in her article "America's Original Sin: Slavery and the Legacy of White Supremacy," "Whiteness still amounted to a value, unmoored from economic or social status. Blackness still had to be devalued, by some in society, to ensure white superiority." This president resembles these remarks based on the parts of society that he constantly attacks (i.e., women, minorities), his obsession with destroying the legacy of President

Obama, as well as his throwing a protective cloak over groups like the clan and the alt-right.

According to a report from the *Washington Post*, the nation's health protection agency is being censored by the Trump administration. How ridiculous can you get? Seven words—*diversity, transgender, evidence-based, science-based, vulnerable, entitlement,* and *fetus*—have reportedly been banned from use at the Center for Disease Control and Prevention in documents related to the 2018 budgets. According to Matt Lloyd, a spokesman for the Department of Health and Human Services, "The assertion that HHS has 'banned words' is a complete mischaracterization of discussions regarding the budget formulation process. HHS will continue to use the best scientific evidence available to improve the health of all Americans. HHS also strongly encourage the use of outcome and evidence data in program evaluations and budget decisions."

How ludicrous can this be for a president to involve himself in such chicanery! Many of these quotes and responses to this mockery are from the experts in their fields. Another quote from an official with Planned Parenthood said, "You cannot fight against the Zika virus or improve women's and fetal health if you are unable to use the word *fetus.* You must be able to talk about science and evidence if you are to research cures for infectious diseases such as Ebola," said Dana Singiser, the organization's vice president of public policy. "You must be able to acknowledge the humanity of transgender people in order to address their health-care needs. You cannot erase health inequities faced by people of color simply by forbidding the use of words like *vulnerable* or *diversity.*"

This is not the first time, according to the report, that this Trump administration has moved toward an oligarchy, a small group of people having control of a country, organization, or institution. They previously tried to control how certain agencies communicated with the public, tailoring their message to fit their agenda. On March 15, 2016, Zynubus wrote the definition of *black soul.* I took those words and related them to America by saying, "The true culture of Americans and the legendary legacy left behind is starting to bring the country to its knees. There is pride, unconscious expression of hope, glory, and passion hidden inside of all of us." Mr. Trump has a black soul because he lacks the capacity for empathy and compassion. He has shown it time and time again with his tweets about women, minorities, and transgender citizens.

If you remember the DNC, Khizr Khan, the father of a Muslim US soldier slain in Iraq in 2004, said that Donald Trump has a black soul, indicating he lacks empathy and compassion. He told CNN's Jim Acosta on *State of the Union* that he hopes Trump's family will "teach him some empathy." "He is a black soul, and this is totally unfit for the leadership of this country," Khan said. "The love and affection that we have received affirms that our grief, that our experience in this country has been correct and positive. The world is receiving us like we have never seen. They have seen the blackness of his character, of his soul."

The outgoing president, Barack Obama, was the target of eight years of pent-up hate even though he assumed the position with the country on the verge of a deep recession from the Bush years. He inherited a Congress that embarrassed and placed the country on the verge of fiscal bankruptcy, totally refused to work across the aisles with this president whether because of race, politics, or both. For the first time in recorded history, one of Congress's Republican senators, Joe Wilson of South Carolina, angrily called President Obama a liar while Congress was in session. That was hate, not politics. You would have expected some type of apology or censure from his Republican colleagues, but not this time. Had it been a Democrat who behaved in a similar manner, they would burn him or her at the stake.

The GOP actually made it perfectly clear that their objective was not to do what was best for the country but to unseat the first black president, which none of them thought had a snowball's chance in hell to win the White House. This is a failure of moral leadership of those elected by their constituents to do what is best for the country and not their personal tyranny. Undoubtedly, President Obama was one of the most disrespected president in this country's history. Hate can be as powerful as love if left unchecked. It's the finger in the dike that is a temporary fix. Even if you are successful in maintaining closure of one breach, the pressure will cause another breach to be exposed.

Laws are not just made by you writing them down; they are made by your actions in carrying them out. If your actions are counter to the written law and are consistently applied, the actions, at some point, become the law. Hate is spontaneous, and it festers over time. Hate is a learned behavior and tends to metastasize over time if left unchecked. It tends to spread from one part of the body (the mind) to another, from your behaviors to your actions. The problem that is created with the metastasis is, it tends to spread to others whom you may have some influence. This may cause them to behave in a way that is consistent with the original tumor, which could be *you*. Where do we go from here?

Some uninformed critics would go as far as saying that President Obama was the worst of any prior individuals gracing the Oval Office. What country were they living in? Let's fact-check these delusionary critics:

- Businesses "added 13.7 million new jobs over a sixty-nine-month streak of job growth."
- More Americans getting health insurance coverage. The rate of the uninsured in America dropped below 10 percent for the first time ever. All in all, 17.6 million people and climbing have gained coverage as the Affordable Care Act has taken effect.
- America's global leadership on climate change.
- In August, the US reopened its embassy in Cuba, the first symbolic step to normalizing relations between the two countries and the first time the

American flag has flown in Havana in fifty-four years.

- In July 2016, six world powers, including the United States, struck a landmark nuclear deal with Iran. And in the months after, despite staunch Republican objection, the deal survived a vote in Congress.
- Standing strong against terrorism.
- In October, Mr. Obama's legacy-defining trade deal involving twelve Pacific Rim countries was sealed, with provisions to cut trade barriers, protect labor and environmental interests, and ensure intellectual property rights.
- In an era where partisan bickering in Washington has reached a fever pitch, the president chose to highlight two bipartisan legislative achievements. He pointed to a sweeping education overhaul of "No Child Left Behind" and a budget deal that avoided the threat of a government shutdown.
- The legalization of same-sex marriage.
- Keeping America safe. Tracking down many of the world's most dangerous terrorist–in particular, Osama bin Laden.
- Regulation of Wall Street without killing the stock market.
- Extended the Bush tax cuts in 2010.

Were there failures during his eight years? Sure, there were. But many of the failures can be traced back to a Congress both Democrat and Republican who refused to support this president for the wrong reasons. Though I am a complete supporter of the Obama administration, there are always those areas that fall short on the expectations of the majority of the country.

Let's consider some of the failures under President Obama:

- The mass murder in Syria–the extent of which is yet to be known will be a permanent stain on Obama's record.
- Short of military action or regime collapse, Iran will have nuclear weapons capability. Obama snubbed the Green Movement, dragged his feet on sanctions, talked down the military option, and failed to isolate Iran diplomatically.
- The deterioration of the US-Israel relationship.
- Black and Latino unemployment continued to spiral out of control. Not all his administration's fault. The economy was in desperate shape from prior administrations.

You can understand now the reason that I put pen to paper on this project. White, black, and brown people are again embroiled in misunderstanding one another's life direction–some based on lack of education and knowledge of the specifics of a culture, and others because of the suffocating hate and racism that has embedded itself in the sick and perverted minds of those Hillary Clinton calls deplorable. As negative as the word seems, it most aptly applies to those who mentally desert reality and enter a realm of belief that everything is bad if it's different. These are many of the same people who didn't know that Obamacare and the Affordable Care Act (ACA) are one and the same.

The Obama era brought pride on the part of blacks and people of color and insecurity on the part of those who never envisioned a black image gracing the White House and sitting in the Oval Office. Hate groups tripled in numbers under President Obama primarily because of those who sought to paint him with a brush of wanting to take away their First Amendment rights. President Obama's ascension to the highest office in the land has uncovered pent-up racism on the part of legislators, law enforcement, the Supreme Court, and many in the general public.

Okay, you don't want to be confused with the facts, so the election is behind us and what do we have . . . President Trump? I leave a pause right here because the country that you and I love just may be in a bit of trouble. We have a president who has no political experience/ expertise, has no real interest in governing, surprised himself that he won the election, lacked the patience to set through security briefings, was allegedly in bed with our Russian advisories, has no clue of the international ramifications of his statements or decisions, has fired half of his appointees in the first six months, wanted to pull out of the Paris Accords–should I go on?

Now there were those Obama critics, who didn't give President Obama the time of day, who are now saying, "Give President Trump a chance. After all, he is our president." Where were these individuals when President Obama needed to be given a chance? Could this be implied or implicit bias, the attitudes or stereotypes that affect our understanding, actions, and decisions in an unconscious and conscious manner? This type of bias is considered to be far more pervasive than conscious bias or prejudice and, in many cases, is in conflict with one's values and beliefs.

It does not give me a lot of satisfaction to criticize the person sitting in the most powerful world position, but respect is earned and not legislated. The danger that this egotistical presidency brings, in my opinion, is a person who is more concerned about his businesses and personal brand than he is about the well-being of this great country. He has a short attention span, a disdain for details, and a feeling that the world is his reality show. He has alienated our allies, embraced our enemies, brought nepotism to the White House, lied continuously about everything that did not cast him in a positive light, and fired the head of the FBI, James Comey, who was investigating his alleged wrongdoings. He has surrounded himself with billionaires and millionaires who do not understand the pulse of the middle class and definitely not the poor and threatened to take millions of people who are now insured under the Affordable Care Act off the insurance rolls, all in the name of cutting taxes for the top 1 percent of the population.

As of this writing, 90 percent of lawmakers are male, 89 percent in the House of Representatives and 93 percent in the Senate. The US population is hovering around 12 percent African American, 9 percent Latino, and 3 percent Asian/Pacific Islanders and others. There has been somewhat of a trend toward the positive with the new changes in Congress in 2019, which is 80 percent white, 80 percent male, and 92 percent Christian. Trump's cabinet is 16 percent female, 7 percent black, and 77 percent white male. Can we surmise that these numbers are an indication of a significant change? I think not. Under President Obama, there were 43 percent white male, 17 percent white female, 13 percent Asian, 8 percent Latino, and 18 percent black.

His cabinet, which is more white and male since Ronald Reagan and beyond rich (the majority), consists of Trump himself (3.7 billion); Mike Pence, vice president ($211,000); Reince Priebus (1.2 million); Jeff Sessions, attorney general (7.5 million); Dr. Ben Carson, secretary, Health and Human Services (26 million); James "Mad Dog" Mattis, secretary of defense (10.6 million); Rex W. Tillerson (365 million); Ryan Zinke, secretary of the interior (675,000); Sonny Perdue, secretary of agriculture (53 million); Wilbur Ross, secretary of commerce (2.5 billion); R. Alexander Acosta, secretary of labor (1.0 million); Rick Perry, secretary of energy (3.0 million), Tom Price, secretary, Health and Human Services (13.6 million); Elaine L. Chao, secretary of transportation (16.9 million); Betsy DeVos, secretary of education (1 billion); David J. Shulkin, Veteran Affairs; John F. Kelly, Homeland Security (456,000); Mike Pompeo, head of the CIA (500,000); Nikki Haley, United Nations (165,000); Scott Pruitt, head of the EPA ($551,000); Linda

McMahon, Small Business (1.35 billion); Mick Mulvaney, Office of Management and Budgets (2.6 million); Dan Coats, director of national intelligence (22.5 million); Robert Lighthizer, US Trade representative (73 million); Kevin Hassett, CEA; Steve Mnuchin, secretary of the treasury (46 million); Andrew Puzder (several million); Steve Bannon, counselor to the president, (54 million); Kellyanne Conway, counselor to the president (44 million); Mike Pompeo, CIA director (456,000); Sean Spicer, press secretary (8.5 million); and Jared Kushner, senior adviser to the president (735 million).

These staggering numbers are in comparison to President Obama's cabinet, which had a net worth of less than 3 billion, and George W. Bush's cabinet was worth just $390 million collectively. Donald Trump's cabinet is worth 13.1 billion, which averages more than the gross domestic product of about sixty five to seventy small countries. Bottom line, we have to get this massive monetary influence out of the political affairs of this country. I do believe in giving a chance to those who deserve or have earned it. This is definitely not the case with this administration. Money and wealth should not be the determining factor in whether a person has a soul, a conscience, and is conscientious in his/her department.

It's not set in stone that people in higher socioeconomic brackets are insensitive to the needs of the middle and lower class, but it's a good bet that most are not. These are the individuals making decisions that will have long-term impact on the lives of the majority of the country. Just as a reference point, the average wage in the United

States is $48,000 as of this writing in June of 2018. That wage index has only gone up by $16,000 since the year 2000.

If the average cost of living increase runs about 3 percent per year, progress against wage inflation has been minimal. The inflation since 2010 has run approximately 10.5 percent. Based on information from the US Census Bureau, since 2007, the year before the most recent recession, real median household income has declined 6.4 percent and is 7.1 percent below the median household income peak that occurred prior to the 2001 recession in 1999. The percentages are not statistically different from one another.

Among racial groups, real median income declined for white and black households between 2009 and 2010, while changes for Asian- and Hispanic-origin households were not statistically different. Real median income for each race and Hispanic-origin groups has not yet recovered to the pre-2001 recession all-time highs. Households in the Midwest, South, and West experienced declines in real median income between 2009 and 2010. The apparent change in median household income for the northeast was not statistically significant.

CHAPTER 11

Neutron Trump

I predict future happiness for Americans, if they can prevent the government from wasting the labors of the people under the pretense of taking care of them.

–Thomas Jefferson

I STARTED THIS project a few months before President Trump was sworn in as the forty-fifth president of the United States. Since that time and considering what was shared in the previous paragraphs, the following appointments are no longer in the White House and part of this administration. Naturally, there are a variety of reasons why people leave jobs or are fired, but what we are experiencing in this administration is disorganized chaos. If you consider the true definition of the word *chaos,* it means "disorder, disarray, disorganized, confusion, mayhem, bedlam, pandemonium, havoc, turmoil, tumult, commotion, disruption, upheaval, uproar maelstrom; behavior so unpredictable as to appear random." In other words, we are experiencing the epitome of unorganized chaos. Prove me wrong.

This administration has more first-year departures than any other president in the last forty-plus years, and the back door is swinging wider every day. Some turnover is expected; however, this is an embarrassment to the country and should be to the president, but it's not because he doesn't care. He is using the office of the presidency as his own reality show.

For you doubters, both Presidents Bush and Obama had similar numbers for some of the key players who left office, but the reasons and processes were different. These men were personally involved when their key figures were fired, and the affected persons did not have to get the news through Twitter, memo, or from another staff member.

➢ Rex Tillerson, US secretary of state, started February, 1, 2017, and left March 13, 2018 (406 days). The secretary of state was apparently "blindsided" while reading about his firing on Twitter after clashing with Trump on several foreign policy matters, including the negotiations with North Korea.

➢ John McEntee, President Trump's personal aide, started January 20, 2017, and left March 12, 2018 (417 days). He was fired as part of the Tillerson move.

- Gary Cohn, director of National Economic Council and chief economic adviser to the president, started January 20, 2017, and left March 6, 2018 (411 days). Resigned after helping Trump implement the tax overhaul. Reported to have resigned over his disagreement with Trump's tariff decisions.
- Hope Hicks, White House communications director, started January 20, 2017, and left office on February 28, 2018 (405 days). Resigned. She is said to be Trump's most loyal aide, resigned the day after testifying before the House Intelligence Committee over the Russia probe.
- Rob Porter, White House staff secretary, started January 20, 2017, and left February 7, 2018 (384 days). Resigned over a domestic abuse scandal that went public. This launches weeks of controversy over Chief of Staff John Kelly's handling of the situation, including when he knew of the allegations against Porter.
- Omarosa Manigault-Newman, director of communications, started January 20, 2017, and left December 13, 2017 (366 days). Resigned. The former *Apprentice* star was reportedly escorted off White House grounds after being fired over her drama.
- Dina Powell, deputy national security adviser, started January 20, 2017, and left January 12, 2018 (358 days). Resigned without fanfare after helping to implement Trump's Middle East policy, including his insistence on moving the US

Embassy in Israel to Jerusalem, which was almost universally condemned during a UN vote.

➤ Tom Price, secretary, Health and Human Services, started February 10, 2017, and left September 29, 2017 (232 days). Resigned after Trump declared that he was not happy over mounting controversy over Price spending $400,000 on private jets for government business (mixed with private use) on the taxpayer's dime.

➤ Sebastian Gorka, deputy assistant to the president on terrorism, started January 30, 2017, and left August 25, 2017 (208 days). Resigned with a scathing letter that criticized Trump's administration direction.

➤ Steve Bannon, chief strategist and senior counsel, started November 13, 2016, and left August 18, 2017 (211 days). Fired. The proud nationalistic chief strategist weathered multiple rounds of ousting rumors while exercising a considerable amount of influence on the president. Trump seemed fed up with his headline grabbing and let him go.

➤ Anthony Scaramucci, communications director, started July 26, 2017, and left July 31, 2017 (6 days). Resigned after giving several controversial television appearances and initiating a reign of terror for a short period in the White House. He did not leave quietly.

➤ Reince Priebus, chief of staff, started January 20, 2017, and left July 28, 2017 (190 days). Resigned after being declared a marked man and a leaker by Scaramucci. He was appraised of his firing when

Trump announced his replacement. He was also forced to depart without access to his office files for fear of other leaks.

➢ Sean Spicer, White House press secretary, started January 20, 2017, and left July 21, 2017 (183 days). Resigned because he was unhappy in the position and was once discovered hiding in the bushes to avoid questions concerning other staff firings. Shortly afterward, he bolted from a press briefing. He resigned after being passed over in favor of Anthony Scaramucci.

➢ Mike Dunkle, communications director, started March 6, 2017, and left May 18, 2017 (74 days). Resigned.

➢ James Comey, FBI director, started under the prior administration September 4, 2013, and left May 9, 2017 (1,344 days). Fired. Trump axed the FBI director in a shocking announcement that even Comey thought was a joke.

➢ Mike Flynn, national security adviser, started January 20, 2017, and left February 13, 2017 (25 days). Resigned after mounting reports that he was vulnerable to Russian blackmail. He has since worked out a deal with the special prosecutor Robert Mueller and pleaded guilty of lying to the FBI.

➢ Sally Yates, acting attorney general, started January 20, 2017, and left January 30, 2017 (11 days). Hired by Obama but fired for not upholding Trump's travel ban on Muslim-majority countries.

- ➤ Katie Walsh, deputy chief of staff, left March 30, 2017 (70 days). Resigned. Departed amid a shake-up, choosing to become an adviser for the Republican National Committee and pro-Trump super PAC, America First Policies.
- ➤ K. T. McFarland, deputy national security adviser, left April 9, 2017 (80 days). Resigned. Left her post after reportedly being asked to do so and subsequently became the US ambassador to Singapore.
- ➤ Vivek Murthy, surgeon general (95 days). Resigned.
- ➤ Angella Reid, White House chief usher (106 days). Dismissed for reasons that are unclear to her at the time, although Axios reports that she was considered mean by staffers.
- ➤ Tera Dahl, deputy chief of staff for the National Security Council (168 days). Reason unknown.
- ➤ Walter Shaub, Office of Government Ethics, left July 6, 2017 (181 days). Resigned. He was the government's chief watchdog. Resigned after several clashes with members of the administration and the president.
- ➤ Mark Corallo, spokesman and communications strategist for the legal team, left July 20, 2017 (50 days). Resigned (183 days) amid disagreements on how to defend the president against Robert Mueller's investigation.
- ➤ Michael Short, assistant press secretary, left July 25, 2017 (187 days). Resigned after Scaramucci

claimed that he would fire the senior assistant press secretary for leaking to reporters.

➢ Derek Harvey, National Security Council adviser (183 days). Fired.

➢ George Gigolos, director of scheduling (193 days). Resigned.

➢ Ezra Cohen-Watnick, senior director of intelligence for the National Security Council, left August 2, 2017 (195 days). Fired by General H. R. McMaster in an apparent attempt to clear out appointees of Michael Flynn. He was shuffled to another position within the administration.

➢ Carl Icahn, special adviser to regulatory reform, left August 20, 2017 (211 days). Resigned.

➢ Keith Schiller, director of Oval Office operations (244 days). Resigned. The billionaire Trump adviser cited an alleged conflict of interest while resigning from his role. He denied insider trading after suspiciously dumping $31 million in steel shares ahead of Trump's tariff announcement.

➢ George Sifakis, assistant to the president and director of the Office of Public Affairs (209 days). Resigned.

➢ Rick Dearborn, deputy chief of staff, left after 347 days. Reason unknown. Now working in the private sector.

➢ Jeremy Katz, deputy director of the National Economic Council, left after 309 days. Resigned.

➢ Dina Powell, deputy national security adviser, left December 8, 2017, after 354 days. Resigned.

➢ Andrew McCabe, FBI deputy director, left March 16, 2018 (375 days). Fired. Went on a permanent leave a few months ahead of his planned retirement. His departure followed months of needling from Trump, including how the president reportedly told McCabe to ask his wife "how it feels to be a loser." His leave was preemptively cut short by Trump on March 16 when he was fired mere days before his pension was to kick in.

➢ Taylor Weyeneth, deputy chief of staff, left after 215 days. Resigned.

➢ Brenda Fitzgerald, director of US Centers for Disease Control and Prevention, left after 209 days. Resigned.

➢ David Sorensen, speechwriter, left after 285 days. Resigned over domestic abuse allegations.

➢ John Feeley, US ambassador to Panama, left after 414 days. Resigned.

➢ John Dowd, Trump's lead lawyer (279 days). Resigned.

➢ Josh Raffel, deputy communications director, left February 27, 2018. Reason unknown. Ivanka Trump was unhappy with his departure.

➢ Rachel Brand, associate attorney general, left February 16, 2018 (268 days). Resigned. As a third-ranking official in the Justice Department's Russia probe, Brand's departure could have wide-ranging effects on the future of Robert Mueller's investigation.

- H. R. McMaster, national security adviser, left March 22, 2018 (362 days). Resigned after numerous clashes with the president. He was replaced by John Bolton.
- Preet Bharara, US attorney, left March 11, 2017. Fired after refusing to submit his resignation to the attorney general.
- Mike Dubke, communications director, left May 18, 2017. Resigned amid rumors of an impending shake-up.

There were other notable departures such as David Shulkin, secretary of Veteran Affairs; Tom Bossert, Homeland Security adviser; Nick Ayers, chief of staff; Michael Anton, NSC spokesperson; Ty Cobb, White House counsel; Josh Raffel, deputy communications director; Scott Pruitt, EPA administrator; Don McGahn, White House counsel; Nikki Haley, United Nations ambassador; Jeff Sessions, attorney general; John Kelly, White House chief of staff; Ryan Zinke, secretary of interior; and Mira Ricardel, deputy national security adviser. The most notable of the departures is John Kelly, White House chief of staff, who started July 28, 2017, and departed at the end of 2018 because he was done with not being able to affect change. Also, there was Jeff Sessions, whom I have little love for because of his historic racial political positions in Alabama, but Trump even misused and abused one who was 110 percent in his corner. I won't belabor this, but I have to mention Michael Cohen. Michael Dean Cohen was President

Trump's personal attorney who was a lawyer for Donald Trump from 2006 until he was relieved of his duties in May of 2018 for lying to Congress.

Cohen was a vice president of the Trump Organization and was often described by many in the media as Trump's fixer. He previously served as copresident of Trump Entertainment and was a board member of the Eric Trump Foundation, a children's health charity. From 2017 to 2018, Cohen was deputy finance chairman of the Republican National Committee.

Trump employed him until May 2018, a year after the Special Counsel investigation into Russian interference in the 2016 United States elections began. The investigation led him to plead guilty on August 21, 2018, to eight counts, including campaign finance violations, tax fraud, and bank fraud.

Cohen said he violated campaign finance laws at the direction of Trump and "for the principal purpose of influencing" the 2016 presidential election. In November 2018, Cohen entered a second guilty plea for lying to a Senate committee about efforts to build a Trump Tower in Moscow.

In December 2018, he was sentenced to three years in federal prison and ordered to pay a $50,000 fine. He reported to prison on May 6, 2019 (Wikipedia). Believe, there is more to come as Cohen continues to testify before Congress prior to his jail sentencing. I am sure another book can be written on the results and effects his testimony will have on the Trump administration.

There are many other departures that are not included in this exhaustive list of people either abandoning their positions or being fired because of loyalty issues. It's indicative of a failed vetting process, an inexperienced president, political finger-pointing, ignorance to the process of hiring and nepotism, and most of all, many are finding out how their brands are being affected as a result of being in this failed administration. With the exception of a few remaining positions who are constantly on pins and needles having to deal with this erratic leader, the administration is in the 90 percent on turnover percentage, which was unheard of in prior administrations. This is the result of a leader who claims to know more than anyone, disregards protocol, scans over details in briefings, and spends most of his day watching Fox News, tweeting about football players kneeling, playing at golf, or testing his popularity among his followers. The next sign that this president is one brick shy of a full load will be his having an imaginary friend because no one else wants the job.

CHAPTER 12

Unconscious Bias

Race is not a biological construct but a social one that can have devastating effects. So many of the horrors of the past few centuries can be traced to the idea that one race is inferior to another. Racial distinctions continue to shape our politics, our neighborhoods, and our sense of self.

—Elizabeth Kolbert

*U*NCONSCIOUS BIAS REFERS to a bias that we are unaware of and which happens outside of our control. It is a bias that happens automatically and is triggered by our brain making quick judgments and assessments of people and situations, influenced by our background, cultural environment, and decisions. This type of bias is odorless and colorless yet lethal. Unconscious bias tends to creep into every fiber of our lives.

We are a very homogenous people as a whole, and unconsciously, we tend to gravitate to people who look like us, act like us, think like us, and come from similar backgrounds. If you ask the average person, they feel that they are open to others' beliefs and ideas, but research has shown that the beliefs and values gained from family, culture, and a lifetime of experiences heavily influence how we view and evaluate both others and ourselves.

Alpha particles and gamma rays bombard us most of our lives, shaping how we think, believe, and act. How we think and assume, whether wrong or right, can be biases. These biases have built up over time and help us to process information quickly and efficiently. From a survival standpoint, bias is a positive and necessary trait. In business, however, bias can be costly. It can cause us to make decisions that are not objective, and ultimately, we miss opportunities. We form opinions about people from first sight, and if our assumptions are fairly correct, we deal with that individual in the proper manner. If the assumptions are not correct, then we shortchange the relationship, and both parties lose a relationship opportunity.

Under a similar category, there is the terminology of *implicit bias*. An implicit bias, or implicit stereotype, is the unconscious attribution of particular qualities to a member of a certain social group. Implicit stereotypes are influenced by experience and are based on learned associations between various qualities and social categories, including race or gender. Individuals' perceptions and behaviors can be affected by implicit stereotypes, even without the individuals' intention or awareness. Implicit bias is an aspect of implicit social cognition–the phenomenon that perceptions, attitudes, and stereotypes operate without conscious intention.

The existence of implicit bias is supported by a variety of scientific articles in the psychological literature. Implicit stereotypes were first defined by psychologists Anthony Greenwald and Mahzarin Banaji in 1995. Explicit stereotypes are the result of intentional, conscious, and controllable thoughts and beliefs. Explicit bias are usually directed toward a group of people based on what is being perceived.

Implicit biases are associations learned through past experiences. Implicit bias can be activated by the environment and operated outside of intentional conscious cognition. For example, we can unconsciously form a bias toward all black horses because they are always portrayed usually as high-spirited and aggressive. This bias may be associated with what we have observed in the movies or on television, but the source of these associations may be misidentified or even unknown by the individual who holds them and can persist even when an individual rejects the bias explicitly.

The myth that black and brown people should not or could not perform in a top leadership position in government, business, and even sports has been dispelled with the crowning of the nation's first black president, Barack Obama; Andy Young, past ambassador to the

United Nations; and Congressman John W. Thompson, chairman, Microsoft Corporation; Kenneth C. Frazier, chairman and CEO, Merck & Co. Inc.; Ursula M. Burns, chairperson and CEO, Xerox Corporation; and the list goes on.

In sports, there is a list of great quarterbacks who just happen to be black like Warren Moon of the Houston Oilers, Doug Williams of the Washington Redskins, Russell Wilson of the Seattle Seahawks, and more. These men and women are examples of why sick-minded individuals were dead wrong with the assertion that blacks could not perform at those levels and particularly in those lofty positions. Now that some of those roadblocks are cleared, what are the new hurdles that will be placed in the lanes of those who are considered different?

This work will not solve the issues at hand but expose the true reality that some are afraid to tackle and others choose to turn a blind eye. Martin Luther King said that "men fear each other because they don't know each other." I shudder when I see innocent men, mostly black and brown, murdered in the streets by those who have sworn to "serve and protect." I would surely feel unsafe if law enforcement was not present, so please don't see these comments as an affront to those who have one of the most difficult jobs in the country next to the military. But even those sworn to uphold the law have vigilantes in their ranks. There is a "blue line of dedication" that those wearing the uniform are sworn to protect whether for the good or bad.

From Ferguson, Missouri, to Los Angeles, California, the news was continually dim of unarmed black and brown men gunned down by those paid to protect us. Why? Usually out of fear, hate, or a lack of sensitivity training–sometimes all of the above. It seems that the predominate law of those patrolling our streets is to shoot first and cover it up under the guise of "I felt threatened." You all remember the "stand your ground" law in Florida, which only works for those they chose to apply the law on their behalf. We remember the Trayvon Martin case where that law was a travesty of justice. Then came the case of Marissa Alexander, a Florida woman who once had been sentenced to twenty years in a case that invoked the state's "stand your ground" law.

Marissa Alexander of Jacksonville, Florida, was accused of firing what she said was a warning shot at her husband and two of his children during a domestic dispute in 2010. She was charged with three counts of aggravated assault with a deadly weapon, convicted, and sentenced under Florida's mandatory minimum guidelines. Alexander's legal team used the "stand your ground" law as part of her legal defense. The law, as the Associated Press puts it, "Says, individuals have no duty to retreat from a place where they have a right to be and may use any level of force, including lethal, if they reasonably believe they face an imminent and immediate threat of serious bodily harm or death." Alexander's case prompted accusations of racial disparity in the application of "stand your ground." This was a summary of the case as presented by NPR. Justice cannot wear a color scale.

Why did "stand your ground" work for George Zimmerman but not for Ms. Alexander? Mr. Zimmerman very well could have embraced an unconscious bias when he stalked Trayvon Martin and later shot him to death simply because of his perceptions of young black men who wear hoods. Unfortunately, we know now that it was just racism based on many of his actions since then and his espoused beliefs. Though he had always wanted to be in law enforcement, like other policemen, and he used the go-to phrase "I felt threatened," that tends to work 100 percent of the time when there is an unjust murder of a black or brown citizen.

In most of the covered incidents where officers used the "I felt threatened" excuse, there were two to three other officers present. There were options to use other weapons at their disposal such as nightsticks, Tasers, or even shoot to wound, not kill. In the case of most blacks, the first option seems to be shoot to kill. Much of the decision has to do with fear, lack of emergency training, and yes, hate. Many officers are not thoroughly screened on their attitudes toward diversity, toward people of color who just don't fit their schema of how things are supposed to be. Many grew up believing that there is something wrong with black. Black hats are worn by the villain in movies; a black cat crossing your path means years of bad luck; Black Friday sales mean that you get something less than it will normally cost; bad things tend to happen in the dark of night. People could just take black in a positive light, such as most black tie/tuxedo affairs are classy; if you are in the black financially, you are in a good place. The idea of casting a group of people in a positive light tends to influence a more civil behavior toward them.

I contend that it is virtually impossible to apply equal justice without holistic respect applied equally among the races. We as parents need to sow the seeds of there being two sides to the color wheel, both good and bad. Good and bad don't always have to denote racial connotations. Black is the absence of light or color, and I, being a black man, hopefully shine brightly to those around me. I try my best to lighten up other's lives when I have the chance, and I certainly am not without color. It sickens me to hear our young people trivialize the *N*-word without thinking of its meaning to those who have had it as an anvil around their necks for hundreds of years.

The younger generation and the hip-hop culture see it as a term of endearment toward those within our race and don't see the residual effects it has outside of the culture. They use the word as a synonym, which is a word or phrase that means exactly or nearly the same as another word or phrase in the same language. Though spelled the same, the *N*-word has a different meaning to those of the baby boomer and gen X generation than those in the millennial generation. It carries the scars of slavery, Jim Crow, deprivation, and racism that some millennials feel that they had yet to experience. I say to those who feel that way as my father once said to us, "Just live on."

Is it unconscious bias when the president can say what he wants without having to be held accountable? No, it's conscious bias on his part and those who chose to play partisan politics. Could Obama have said the things that Trump has said without impeachment? Consider this: Bill Cosby, actor; Ben Affleck, actor; Oliver Stone, writer; Bob Weinstein, producer; Kevin Spacey, actor; Steven Seagal, actor; Al Franken, politician; Russell Simmons, producer; Charlie Rose, journalist; etc.–these men were accused of harassment, and many have experienced massive negative hits to their income and ability to work. If convicted, then all should have to pay the price, including Mr. President himself. Are you telling me that sixteen women are all lying about his harassment?

This "do nothing" Congress and House fail to act because it's their party under attack. Trump said during the campaign that he could stand and shoot a gun down Fifth Avenue in New York and not lose any votes. I think he was right. His hard-core base doesn't really care what he does as long as someone like Obama is not in the White House.

A two-party system is a system where two major political parties dominate politics within a government. One of the two parties typically holds a majority in the legislature and is usually referred to as the majority party, while the other is the minority party. Is it time to look at whether there needs to be a change in both party majority system as well as the Electoral College? The current state of affairs is what happens when a government loses its soul. It's party over country, black, Latino, Asian, and poor versus white. Is this what we really want? The alt-right and the neo-Nazi groups would love to have a race war. Is that where we are headed? Are we headed for an oligarchy where only a few at the top rule as was the case in South Africa under apartheid?

Apartheid was a system of institutionalized racial segregation and discrimination in South Africa between 1948 and 1991. Broadly speaking, apartheid was delineated into petty apartheid, which entailed the segregation of public facilities and social events, and grand apartheid, which dictated housing and employment opportunities by race.

Prior to the 1940s, some aspects of apartheid had already emerged in the form of minority rule by white South Africans and the socially enforced separation of black South Africans from other races, which later extended to pass laws and land apportionment. Apartheid was adopted as a formal policy by the South African government after the ascension of the National Party during the country's 1948 general elections according to Wikipedia.

Can you see the similarities in what this administration is doing with the appointments to the Supreme Court, the support of racism in high position, and the makeup of President Trump's cabinet with the likes of Jeff Sessions, Rick Perry, and Steve Bannon? Look at the people he respects, who are all primary dictators like Putin in Russia and Xi Jinping of China. He believes in loyalty beyond reason. He is obsessed with self-aggrandizement. He worries about what is going on in the NFL, statue replacement, crowd size, reliving the election, and nepotism over what's right for the country. You may not have been an Obama supporter, but there are many now who wish they had their vote back.

CHAPTER 13

Our History: Why the Word Negro

If any man claims the Negro should be content . . . then let him say he would willingly change the color of his skin and go to live in the Negro section of a large city. Then and only then has he a right to such a claim.

—Robert Kennedy

I THINK IT is necessary to demystify the term *Negro*. Why do President Trump, the courts, law enforcement, and white females always seem to think negatively about those who look different from what they are comfortable and familiar with? I have sometimes consumed that kool aide, and I am a black male.

I have primarily lived in affluent neighborhoods, so seeing someone from across the tracks, as we say, can create unconscious bias. I have crossed the street or darted into a nearby store when a group of young black men were coming toward me using loud and aggressive voices. We demonize young black men in the news media, in the penal system, and in the courts enough to create unconscious bias even in people coming from the same generation and culture.

White females sometimes cross the street or grab their purses when there is a black male close by. In the grocery store, I have observed white women clutch their purses when I push my basket anywhere near theirs. White men can go right up to their carts with a significantly different reaction because of the homogeneity effect. Society and the media have created a fear that most black men have a thuggish gene no matter how they look or which side of the tracks they are from.

Let's briefly discuss the genesis of the word *Negro*. The word *Negro* was traditionally used to denote a person who was black in skin color or was dark complected. It was used by the Spanish and Portuguese and was derived from the Latin word *niger*. The word fell out of favor in the United States during the 1970s as blacks observed other cultures' use of the word. A change took place, and the word *Negro* was used in relation to the more derogatory term such as *nigras*. This rendition of the word was overly used by President Lyndon B. Johnson, and the racist nature of the times eventually migrated the word to *Nigger*.

Older organizations like the United Negro College Fund and the NAACP tended to hold on to the term

Negro because they were led by those born before the post–World War II baby boom. Many older blacks were appalled at the younger generation's preference to use the term *black* instead of *Negro*.

While some argue that prevailing attitudes in this country should not always be taken into account when deciding what words people should use in other languages, others try to avoid using *Negro* or its variants as they have come to consider that it could be possibly offensive. Implementing this decision is not always easy because in some languages, the word for *black* is not considered to be a better alternative at all. Some cultures settle for *dark-skinned* or *African*.

However, many languages presently do not have any widely accepted alternatives for an alternative to *Negro*, which is more neutral or positive in its associations. Some Spanish-speaking people have adopted the term *negrito* or even *azulito* (the diminutive of *azul*, the color blue) instead of *negro* to avoid the insulting connotation of the word in English, especially around English-speaking people who do not know Spanish. A specifically female form of the word—*negress*—was sometimes used, but like another gender-specific word, *Jewess*, it has all but completely fallen from use. Both are considered racist and sexist.

James Brown, the noted entertainer and soulful artist, wrote the song "Say It Loud, I'm Black and I'm Proud," which caught on as a prideful rallying cry for those of us baby boomers. The song was written by Pee Wee Ellis, band leader, in 1968 and performed by none other than the Godfather of Soul, Mr. James Brown. Two (2) of the more remembered lyrics stated:

> Some people say we've got a lot of malice,
> Some say it's a lot of nerve,
> But I say we don't quit moving,
> Until we get what we deserve.
> We've been buked and we have been scorned,
> We've been treated bad, talked about as sure
> as you were born.
> But just as sure as it takes two eyes to make
> a pair,
> Ha brother, we can't quit until we get our
> share.

If you truly want to know our history, there is an interesting story to tell that, just maybe, will assist with that unconscious bias.

From my research and resources such as the African American Registry, I found it interesting that currently in Italy, using the term *Negro* to refer to a black person would be considered a racist insult, suggestive of fascist opinions. Yet in Portuguese, the socially accepted term is *Negro*, while *preto* (meaning "black-skinned") usually is seen as a possible insult because of social color bias. Portuguese people and Portuguese-speaking Africans prefer the term *preto*, in opposition of *blanco* (white), than *Negro*, which to them means "dirty."

Words have deep-rooted connotations based on the perception of the user. For example, the word *diversity* means "a variety or a range of different things, an instance of being composed of different elements or qualities." But those who are not supportive of the word chose to define it as "strictly for minorities and women and carrying an undertone of special treatment and having to accept someone that is 'less than' the norm." Now you can begin to see what the misrepresentation of words and their meanings can have on those having to deal with these attitudes and perceptions.

On another note, there are segments of the political right who honestly believed that black slaves were better off in slavery than free because they had a place to sleep, food to eat, and some form of clothing on their backs. For the most part, slaves' diet consisted of a form of fatty pork and corn or rice. The poor quality and sometimes quantity of food led to slaves that were either sickly or unable to perform at the level expected. Historian U. B. Phillips found that slaves received the following standard with little or no deviation–"a quart of cornmeal and half pound of salt pork per day for each adult and proportionally for children, commuted or supplemented with sweet potatoes, field peas, syrup, rice and fruit." Actually, our diets have not changed significantly primarily in the South. Corn bread, greens, ham hocks, mac and cheese, rice, and black-eyed peas are still what we call a soul food meal.

Many realized that the slaves' diets were quantitatively filling but not qualitatively sufficient to sustain them through grueling hot summer days and cold winters. The poor quality of food led to slaves that were either "physically impaired or chronically ill" according to Eugene Genovese (American South historian). Antebellum plantations had a larger population of hogs than cows, therefore, producing more pork than beef.

There are a few reasons behind having more pigs than cows. There's a stereotype that slaves preferred pork over beef, and beef was harder to preserve, so it was typically only served fresh (which happened more often in the winter because the cold slowed spoiling). There was a fear of fresh meat because it was believed, by the owners, to cause disease among blacks and also the planters' conviction that "hog was the only proper meat for laborers." Due to the lack of cattle consumption and use (other than for fertilizer), another problem that arose among slaves' diets was the absence of milk.

There was often a stereotype in the antebellum South that slaves were lactose intolerant. However, many slaves had trouble digesting lactose (in dairy products) because it was not a common staple in their diets. Due to the scorching summer heat and the poor quality of the animals themselves, milk became a scarce product only available seasonally. When it did become available, it was given to whites first and, if any remained, then to slave children. Additionally, there are some scientific hypotheses behind blacks more often being lactose intolerant than whites today.

The cabins were lit by fires or candles; wind curiously found its way between the logs on cold winter nights. This is 2018, and we still have conservatives in deep, dark red states who long for the days of slavery based on not what they know but what they have been told by their forefathers. Try stepping into the shoes or sandals of those who were under the whip, those who ate what they could but not what was best for them. Think about your family being separated—children from mothers, husbands from wives, sisters from brothers. Think about the rape of our daughters and sisters, the murder of our brothers and fathers or having their limbs removed because they sought freedom from the inhumane treatment of the racist overseers. Are you there in their places? How does it feel? Would you wish to stay in those conditions if you were unfortunate enough to have gone through that terrible period in America's history?

In political, economic, and social categories, racial difference and its consequences remain profoundly real. White privilege has been much on display even today as we observe the current administration's attack on anyone of color. This has become crystal clear as armed white men proclaiming white supremacy marched unmolested in the streets, while unarmed and, most often, innocent black and brown men are shot down by police who are rarely held to account. Politicians run successful campaigns on platforms of racial hatred, succeeding primarily as a result of folding it under the cloak of justice reform when it's really *just us* who bear the brunt of their reform.

Our parents came up during a period of Jim Crow, when the word *Negro* was the accepted term. The actual decline in the use of the word *Negro* started around 1965–1966 when the Black Panther Party and Stokely

Carmichael started to use the term *black power.* Our elders were appalled at the energy that was sweeping the young people during that period and forbade our use of the word *black.* I remember my aunt Evelyn telling me to stop using the word *black* "'cause we's Negros." I loved that lady who was larger than life to me. She was a big woman with an even bigger heart. She believed in evangelists, or tent preachers as they were called. Many a day while visiting her, I would attend these tent sessions with her; and with only a few pieces of change in her pocket, she would give it all to these shysters who knew that they were playing upon the deep-rooted religious beliefs of older folks during that period.

Their dedication to these false prophets fell just short of the Jonestown massacre. The Peoples Temple Agricultural Project, better known by its informal name Jonestown, was a remote settlement established by the Peoples Temple, an American cult under the leadership of Reverend Jim Jones in north Guyana. It became internationally notorious when on November 18, 1978, approximately 918 people died in the settlement at the nearby airstrip in Port Kaituma and at a temple-run building in Georgetown, Guyana's capital city.

Why do I compare what my aunt was doing to worshipping under this form of dominance? It's called mind manipulation. Mind manipulation, also known as mind control, is the ability to manipulate and/or control the minds of other beings. Mind manipulation can be a natural extension of telepathy or accessed through healing. It is not to be mistaken for suggestion, which is the ability to plant thoughts and ideas in the minds of others. These soul snatchers were playing on the vulnerability of elderly parishioners who believed in anyone who carried a Bible. They could say and ask for anything as long as they did it in the name of the Lord.

Now think about another synonym of mind manipulation called brainwashing. Brainwashing is the concept that the human mind can be altered or controlled by certain psychological techniques. Brainwashing is said to reduce its subject's ability to think critically or independently; to allow the introduction of new, unwanted thoughts and ideas into the subject's mind; as well as to change his or her attitudes, values, and beliefs. Now you see where I am going with this. These tent preachers knew exactly what they were doing and their overall objective to influence the minds of those vulnerable to their sleight of hand tactics.

Many of you may laugh at their position on the matter, but understand that it was the sign of the times of that period. It took many years for the word *Negro* to be cleansed after being denigrated by the majority population who chose to replace the *o* in *Negro* with an *a*, coining the word *Negra*. What it actually did was assimilate to a more acceptable term than what was really intended, the word *Nigger*.

First used in the census in 1900, *Negro* became the most common way of referring to black Americans through most of the early twentieth century, during a time of racial inequality and segregation. *Negro* itself had taken the place of *colored*. Starting with the 1960s civil rights movement, black activists began to reject the *Negro* label and came to identify themselves as black or African American.

"Say It Loud, I'm Black and I'm Proud" became a song black people embraced into the fall of 1968, a song of black pride. The words urged black people to stand up for themselves in the midst of the black is beautiful movement that was spreading from urban cities to rural America. Black pride was a movement in response to dominant white cultures and ideologies that encouraged black people to celebrate black culture and embrace their African heritage. In the United States, it was a direct response to white racism especially during the civil rights movement. Related movements include Black Power, black nationalism, Black Panthers, and Afrocentrism. With James Brown and Stokely Carmichael driving the new movement with their activism and music, a new day was dawning.

The Black Panthers, also known as the Black Panther Party, was a political organization founded in 1966 by Huey Newton and Bobby Seale to challenge police brutality against the African American community. Dressed in black berets and black leather jackets, the Black Panthers organized armed citizen patrols of Oakland and other US cities. At its peak in 1968, the Black Panther Party had roughly two thousand members. The organization later declined as a result of internal tensions, deadly shootouts, and FBI counterintelligence activities aimed at weakening the organization. A new fear started to creep into white America because the usual nonviolent movement of Dr. Martin Luther King was not the choice of the younger generation.

At the same time, there were the black Muslims. Black Muslims, African American religious movement in the United States, split since the late 1970s into the American Society of Muslims and the Nation of Islam. The original group was founded (1930) in Detroit by Wali Fard (or W. D. Fard), whom his followers believed to be Allah in person. When Fard disappeared mysteriously in 1934, Elijah Muhammad assumed leadership of the group, first in Detroit and then in Chicago. Under his leadership, the black nationalist and separatist sect (then called the Nation of Islam) expanded, mainly among poor blacks and prison populations. Although the group numbered only about eight thousand when Muhammad took over, it grew rapidly in the 1950s and '60s, particularly as a result of the preaching of one of its ministers, Malcolm X. All these events created a heightened fear factor on the part of white America as well as the Justice Department.

CHAPTER 14

The Black Perspective

It does not matter how long you are spending on the earth, how much money you have gathered or how much attention you have received. It is the amount of positive vibration you have radiated in life that matters.
                    –Amit Ray, Meditation: Insights and Inspirations

RECENTLY IN CHARLOTTE, North Carolina, Jonathan Ferrell was shot to death by law enforcement while looking for help after a car accident. Ferrell, a twenty-four-year-old former Florida A&M football player, crashed his car early Saturday morning. After climbing out, he ran to a nearby home for help. The resident, a woman waiting for her husband, opened the door and–realizing it wasn't him–closed it. She then called 911 to report a man trying to break into her home. Three officers arrived and found Ferrell about a block from the house. During the encounter, according to the police report, Ferrell ran toward them, and at least one opened fire, killing him. Black man down.

Ferrell joins a long, tragic list of unarmed black men losing their lives unnecessarily. Kamani Gray was shot to death on March 10, 2013, by officers in Brooklyn, New York, after he was confronted for "suspicious behavior." A year before, in New Orleans, Wendell Allen, 20, was killed in his home by police executing a search warrant for marijuana. Kendrec McDade, 19, was killed while running from police in Pasadena, California after he was falsely accused of attempted theft.

Now it's tempting to say race had nothing to do with this–that it was a tragic accident borne of fear and misunderstanding. After all, there's no evidence of intentional bias, just a young man in the wrong place at the wrong time. But racism is a cultural force as much as it is a series of beliefs, and as such, it bears on our subconscious as much as it does our actions. For Americans, race has a strong pull on our sense of fear and our perceptions of aggression, a fact that has more to do with the legacy of slavery and our long history of racial demonization than it does any particular set of crime statistics. In particular, according to a range of surveys and implicit association tests, which measure unconscious bias by flashing faces and soliciting responses, white Americans are more afraid of black men than any other group in the country.

In one such test (PDF), researchers found that black males elicited the most negative reactions from white subjects—simply seeing them was enough to make participants feel uncomfortable. And in a 2009 survey on the question of blacks and violence drawn from a nationally representative sample of white Americans, more than 30 percent said that blacks were more violent than whites. Respondents were also asked specifically about violence among black men versus white men, black women, and white women. The results? More than 40 percent said that "many" or "almost all" black men were violent compared to less than 20 percent who said the same of black women or white men and less than 10 percent who said the same of white women. No doubt these conscious biases are fed by stories such as that of Aaron Alexis, the man suspected of killing twelve people and seriously wounding three others at the Southeast Washington Navy Yard, Washington, DC, in September of 2013.

With all this in mind, let's return to the Ferrell shooting, with the reality of unconscious bias in mind. When Ferrell knocked on the door asking for help, did the woman see an injured young man dazed and confused from a car accident? Or did she see someone who would harm her if she didn't take action? Judging from her decision to call the police and report the incident as an attempted burglary, my guess is the latter. It's one thing to ask for police assistance, but it's something else to assume malign intent. Likewise, when the police confronted Ferrell, did they see someone who needed assistance, or did they assume—instinctively—that the young black man coming toward them was someone who was up to no good? A running black man is automatically a target based on society's fear of his motives. I think we know the answer.

None of this is to say that the men and women responsible for Ferrell's death are racists. There's no way to know what lives in their hearts, but my guess is that they aren't the reincarnations of Bull Connor. They don't have to be; this is just how racism works. The idea that African Americans are prone to violence has a long pedigree, from antebellum fears of slave revolts to the 1890s, when white supremacist scholars took crime statistics and twisted them into "proof" of inherent black criminality.

Fear of black men has a tremendous hold on the American subconscious, and it mixes with our perceptions in ways that guarantee tragedy. As a nation, it's one of our deadliest problems, and I'm not sure we can fix it. These names and dates were as a result of an article written by Jamelle Bouie on implicit bias in 2013. Dr. King was right when he said, "Men often hate each other because they fear each other; they fear each other because they don't know each other; they don't know each other because they cannot communicate; they cannot communicate because they are separated." Why do whites fear those who don't look like them? We as a people have limited economic power, we are not major players in the global markets (yet), and we don't own *Fortune* 500 major businesses or control the banking industry, so why the fear? It's simply the fear of the unknown. Don't fear me; engage me, include me, and you will be surprised at the treasures you may find.

From a personal perspective, there was an incident that happened to me in Washington, DC, as I returned from a visit to the campus of Howard University. At the time, I was a member of the prestigious unit called the Old Guard, located in Fort Myer, Virginia. The Old Guard is the army's official ceremonial unit and escort to the president, and it also provides security for Washington, DC, in time of national emergency or civil disturbance. I was running to catch what was the last bus from Virginia to Washington, DC, at approximately 11:15 p.m.

The last bus was to leave a certain point at 11:30 p.m. As I swiftly jogged toward the bus stop, which was quite a distance, a patrol car pulled up beside me and asked what I was running from. I explained that I wasn't running from anything but to catch the bus that was to leave in about ten minutes. Instead of allowing me to continue on and catch my bus because I had done nothing, I was asked to show my ID and proof that I was a member of the Old Guard. I asked, "Why am I being stopped?" The officer on the passenger side, in a very intimidating tone, said, "We ask the questions. You just listen. It's a little suspect that someone like you [implicit bias] is running in this neighborhood unless you are guilty of something." They checked out my ID, stared me up and down once more, and sent me on my way. Wouldn't it have been a nice "protect and serve" behavior to say, "Get in. We will get you to the bus stop on time." That would have left a positive impression in my mind of those officers and the police department even though the prior encounter had happened. Instead, it made me leery of any contact with them no matter the circumstance. I did make the bus only because the bus driver saw me coming in the distance and was kind enough to wait.

There were other similar incidents in Simi Valley, Ventura County, California. I, before retiring as vice president of a major corporation, was driving to a speaking engagement from my home in Simi Valley. As I proceeded up a ramp leading to the SR23 on ramp, I had a flat tire. I pulled safely off the road and stood behind the car, calling AAA, when a patrolman pulled up behind me. As I continued speaking with the dispatcher from AAA, he seemed irritated that I was on the phone. As I finished my conversation, his first words were, "What are you doing over here?" as if to say I didn't belong in the neighborhood.

He was not interested in the trouble I was having but concerned by my presence. My response was, "Why didn't you ask if I needed help instead of questioning my being here?" I realized that I was taking a risk by speaking to him that way, but I felt we were in an open, well-traveled area, so I felt a bit safe versus being on a side street or in the dark. "Sir, I have a flat tire, but you chose not to ask about that. Why?" Once I told him that I was a vice president of a large corporation in the area, his demeanor changed. He then asked if he could help in any way. I said no and that I already had it taken care of. He stayed with me at the scene until AAA arrived. I would like to think that he stayed out of concern, but he and I both knew he stayed to make sure that I left and that I had in fact called AAA.

There was another incident that happened to my son, Marcus, who had, on several occasions, been followed from his employer to our front gate by a local policeman. The patrolman would not leave until he saw Marcus open the gate to our community. I guess seeing him go into a gated community somehow gave him passage. My son, a large black man, driving a Cadillac Escalade, must have gotten his attention.

A few nights later in the same city, Marcus had stopped by a 7-Eleven store to get a cold drink and some Skittles. As he pulled into the parking lot, he was surrounded by local policemen who pulled him out of his car and handcuffed him as he lay on the ground. The store attendant rushed out to the police to let them know my son wasn't the one he had reported. The person in question was a slender young man wearing a cap and jeans. Marcus is 6 feet and weighs 230 lbs. and did not fit the description given by the clerk of the individual causing the problem. See, here again. Some rogue cops hear the word *black*, and any black person in the area becomes a suspect whether they fit the description or not.

Once the officers had spoken to the young man in question, they returned to where Marcus was still handcuffed on the ground. After taking the handcuffs off, Marcus asked for an apology, but the young police officer didn't feel that he had anything to apologize for. Marcus was able to get his name and badge number. After discussing the incident with me, I requested a meeting with the mayor, the police chief, the city manager, and Marcus to discuss the experience. As a result of the meeting, the police chief committed to having his officers attend sensitivity and diversity training. The officer was later reassigned because of his being involved in a similar incident in the past. The correct thing to do was not to reassign him but to terminate him because there was a historic pattern to his behavior.

This is one situation that didn't end tragically but could have. At a later date, I had the opportunity to address the group again and took the opportunity to explain to them that black fathers have different discussions with their sons when they leave home than what a white father has. A black father has to tell his son to obey in every way, keep his hand on the wheel, not be aggressive, follow orders, be respectful, make no sudden moves, stay in the car until instructed otherwise, speak in a pleasant tone, and hope that they live through the experience.

Even following orders does not guarantee our young men that they won't be harmed. A white young man can be belligerent, aggressive, disrespectful, and overbearing, but the chances are great that they will be sent away with the maximum of a ticket and good advice. Most of the outcome is based on the perception of the individual, and unfortunately, race plays a significant part.

There are many current examples of how implicit, or even unconscious, bias is a very visible and front-page subject matter. Take the case of Colin Kaepernick, who, before leaving, was the quarterback for the San Francisco

49ers. It was his intention to redirect the narrative stemming from his recent refusal to stand for the national anthem. What began as a gesture of taking a knee during the playing of the national anthem as a protest to police brutality and social injustice in this country turned into a political football because the president decided that the country's international problems could be put on hold as he called for the removal of all the "sons of bitches" who took a knee in disrespect to the military and our country.

Was Kaepernick disparaging the sacrifices made by the military as some charged? As a black man and Vietnam War veteran, I say, absolutely not. The flag is a symbol of our democracy and does not apply to all cultures equally. The First Amendment allows for the freedom of speech and expression, which Kaepernick demonstrated. Would I have handled it that way? Probably not because I am not in a position to affect as many people as he did with his celebrity status as well as with a national audience looking on. I applaud the brother for using his platform to call attention to a serious social problem of brutality, which somehow got muddled in the bait-and-switch tactics of Trumpism.

I was honored to have heard a speech by Kaepernick, and I am even more supportive of his stance against racism and bigotry. I am impressed that it was not just a flash in the pan and an attempt at self-aggrandizement. He spoke about love, brotherhood, and faith. He spoke about dehumanization norms and how these inhuman beliefs and actions on the part of those in position of service, like the legislature, the police departments, and the courts, seem to have woven hatred into the fabric of the nation. He continued to say that the United States of America has incarcerated the largest prison population in the history of humankind–2.2 million.

Systemic racism is alive and well in America, but many do not see it either because they don't want to or because they don't recognize it because of the rose-colored glasses that color their thinking. We protest not to start problems but instead to bring focus on injustice no matter the race, creed, or color. It was James Baldwin who said, "To be black in America and to be relatively conscious is to be in a rage all of the time. All you are ever told in this country about being black is that it is a difficult road. You have to decide who you are, and force the world to deal with you, not with its idea of you.

"One is born in a white country ... when you open your eyes to the world, everything you see: none of it applies to you. You go to white movies and, like everybody else, you fall in love with Joan Crawford, and you root for the Good Guys who are killing off the Indians. It comes as a great psychological collision when you realize all of these things are metaphors for your oppression, and will lead into a kind of psychological warfare in which you may perish."

Those quotes are deserving of your close scrutiny. The root words in Baldwin's quotes are *relatively conscious, survival, force, recreate*, and *oppression*. When everyone else is running toward the finish line and we are waiting to hear the sound of the pistol, you have already lost the race. You see, in a race where time is critical and a good start gives you a chance at a great finish, most runners know that the smoke comes out of the pistol before the sound; and if you wait on the sound before getting out of the blocks, you have lost the race. People of color seem to be waiting for the sound.

Wake up, America. Kaepernick is a symptom of much larger systemic issues in America. Even a nonpolitical as I am knows that the system is broken. The Electoral College is a sham; gerrymandering is committing fraud against the freedom to vote. Voter registration laws are unfairly applied to the least and the last. We selectively use the First Amendment when it suits us. We stack the courts with conservative bigots who will shape policy for decades to come. We allow powerful individuals to shape our thinking instead of thinking for ourselves. Is this the America we want? I can hear some of you saying a resounding yes, which proves my point that our democracy is under attack.

For our president and the NFL owners to blackball this talented individual and stifle his career because he exercised his right under the First Amendment, shame on you. There are many quarterbacks in the NFL who can't carry Kaepernick's water but are drawing large paychecks. These owners are reacting to their pockets and are afraid that fans will boycott the games. So be it. Let them boycott, and I guarantee that each of them will still have billions in the bank. Greed prevents them from doing the right thing. These massive players are but chattel (personal possession or ownership) to these owners, and recent decisions are living proof of that fact.

President Trump was apoplectic and had declared war on the media who exercised their First Amendment rights. It seems that as long as he and the Congress agree with what is said and demonstrated, things are fine. As soon as they feel that the First Amendment challenges their beliefs, they flip the script, create a smoke screen, create a dog whistle, then bait and switch to get their way like some small child with a pacifier.

There was little to no discussion around the black and brown people being gunned down in the street but more to the president's assertion that the kneeling was disrespectful to our men and women in uniform and the national anthem. I am one of those who were in uniform, but I don't feel disrespected at all. In fact, I am happy that my service served to protect Kaepernick and others' right to free speech. President Trump can't speak for all veterans, specifically this one.

For those who are a little fuzzy on the First Amendment, it states, "The First Amendment to the United States Constitution prohibits the making of any law respecting an establishment of religion, ensuring that there is no prohibition on the free exercise of religion, abridging the freedom of speech, infringing on the freedom of the press, interfering with the right to peaceably assemble, or prohibiting the petitioning for a governmental redress of grievances." It was adopted on December 15, 1791, as one of the ten amendments that constitute the Bill of Rights.

Kaepernick said, "I am not going to stand up to show pride in a flag for a country that oppresses black people and people of color. To me, this is bigger than football, and it would be selfish on my part to look the other way. There are bodies in the street and people getting paid leave and getting away with murder." Were his actions against the law? I think not. Mr. Kaepernick is a fraternity brother of mine as part of Kappa Alpha Psi Fraternity. Am I supporting him for that reason? Maybe, but it has to be because he is within his rights. According to National World News, this is what should be considered. According to Title 36 (Section 171) of the United States Code, "During rendition of the national anthem, when the flag is displayed, all present except those in military uniform *should*, not must, stand at attention facing the flag with the right hand over the heart."

Men not in uniform *should* remove their headdress with their right hand and hold it at the left shoulder, the hand being over the heart. Persons in uniform should render the military salute at the first note of the anthem and retain the position until the last note is rendered. When the flag is displayed, those present should face toward the music. Section 171 does not specify or impose penalties for violating the section of the code. Cases have concluded that the Flag Code does not proscribe conduct but is merely declaratory and advisory.

As of July 2019, Colin has not been offered a position with an NFL team. Does it cause someone like me and others to wonder whether he is being blacklisted among the owners for fear of backlash from their ticket holders, or do they agree with Trump that they should be run out of the league and maybe even the country? Many of these owners see the players as chattel to own and sell as they please. It's servitude at its highest level.

Now the NFL owners have voted to require any player who takes the field during a game to stand for the national anthem. If they don't want to stand, they can stay in the locker rooms until after the anthem is played. Why is that an issue? Because those who choose to remain in the locker room will be singled out by the racist public as a "problem" and ostracized by even some of their fellow teammates. In addition to being humiliated, the individual and/or the team can be fined if there is a demonstration of the First Amendment on the field. Thanks, Mr. Trump, for making a simple protest a divisive issue in direct conflict with what free speech should be about.

Billionaires, when is enough, enough? When will you stand for the right instead of exercising might? When will you stop cherry-picking situations that you will tolerate and those you will not? You have accepted athletes back after serving time for murder, other felonies, and abuse, but you won't stand with a talented young man who is simply exercising his First Amendment rights. You will not consider that there is still not "justice for all." More men of color are being gunned down in the streets when the situation could have been handled with less force. When will the police network stop defending those whom they know are racists? When will our officers stop using the excuse, "I felt threatened," after gunning down defenseless citizens, primarily black and Latino? When will law enforcement properly screen out those who should never wear the uniform because of their values and views?

The point here is, there are perceptions of people of color that drive those in power positions to base individual situations on a racial perception. These perceptions, in many instances, result in the loss of life. We allow perceptions to drive our behavior. If our perception is incorrect, then our behavior is based on an incorrect assumption that can shortchange both individuals as they attempt to communicate with one another. First of all, see me because that signifies the initial respect; then value me, which allows the communication to take place; then get to know me because they could be a nugget at the end of this rainbow.

The sooner we admit that there is police brutality, the sooner there will be a mending of the relationship between the police and the communities. I highly respect law enforcement and would hate to see a country without it, but even Stevie Wonder can see that people of color are being targeted. Until the majority starts to realize that there is a universal responsibility to see justice for all, the current trend will continue. A minor scratch to the surface of this country will expose the racial pressures that have built over time. When there are pressure points building up without a release valve, an explosion is imminent. What happened in Charlottesville, Virginia, is just a symptom of a deeper divide on race in this country.

The pressure started to build over the last eight years under the administration of the first black president, Barack Obama. It was indicative in a statement made by

Senate Majority Leader Mitch McConnell of Kentucky that from day 1, he was determined to make President Obama a one-term president. The statement within itself indicates that he and his colleagues would do nothing to help this president succeed or the country succeed. This man had not had time to warm the chair in the Oval Office when McConnell made the statement. Would he have made the same statement if it was a white Democrat who was elected? I think not.

Then there was the isolated portion of President Obama's address to Congress in which Representative Joe Wilson of South Carolina shouts, "You lie," after Obama says that illegal immigrants would not benefit from his health-care reform plan. Never in the annals of history have a president been as disrespected as President Obama. You can't believe it was because of his policies or his stance internationally. So what? He kept us safe during those eight years, and he made sure that millions of our citizens had insurance.

He represented this country with dignity and class. So what was it? Was it a lack of knowledge of the position? I think not. Was it lack of international experience? I think not. Was it lack of experience dealing with climate change? I think not. So what was it? Was it his race? I personally and unequivocally say a resounding yes. I wonder if that question will ever be answered, so we will be left to speculate on our own. I continue to ask the question, Has America lost its soul?

CHAPTER 15

Fear as a Weapon

There are four ways you can handle fear. You can go over it, under it, or around it. But if you are ever to put fear behind you, you must walk straight through it. Once you put fear behind you. Leave it there.

—Donna Favors

FEAR OF WHAT or who? Fear is an emotion induced by a threat perceived by living entities, which causes a change in brain and organ function and ultimately a change in behavior, such as running away, hiding, or freezing from traumatic events. To shoot an unarmed man through a window in a car—as was done in the Philando Castile case, with a mother and child in the car—was unadulterated fear and perception. Shooting an unarmed man as he ran away, as in the Walter Scott case, is a case of rage and deep-rooted hate. Out of sheer fear, a female officer shot an unarmed man, Terence Crutcher, while three (3) other officers were present. The excuse given was "I thought I was pulling my Taser." Why do our justice system approximately 98 percent of the time buy into the bull presented to them without question when a policeman is involved in the death of a person of color? It's because of perception, hate, fear, and pathological lying. That's right, I said it!

The fear response arises from the perception of danger leading to the confrontation with or the escape from it, avoiding the threat (also known as the fight-or-flight response), which in extreme cases of fear (horror and terror) can be a freeze response or paralysis. In most of the cases, the victims were large black or brown men who were a visual threat within their own right.

According to research on fear, fear can be learned by experiencing or watching a frightening, traumatic accident. For example, if a child falls into a well and struggles to get out, he or she may develop a fear of wells, heights (acrophobia), enclosed spaces (claustrophobia), or water (aquaphobia). There are studies looking at areas of the brain that are affected in relation to fear. When looking at these areas (such as the amygdala), it was proposed that a person learns to fear regardless of whether they themselves have experienced trauma or if they have observed the fear in others.

In a study completed by Andreas Olsson, Katherine I. Nearing, and Elizabeth A. Phelps, the amygdala is affected both when subjects observed someone else being submitted to an aversive event, knowing that the same treatment awaited themselves, and when subjects were subsequently placed in a fear-provoking situation. This suggests that fear can develop in both conditions, not just simply from personal history.

Many stereotypes have been fabricated by those wishing to keep fear as a primary motivator. Also, fear engulfs those who fail to educate themselves and are vulnerable to the masochistic beliefs of those who hate. The mere thought of there potentially being a mixed race of people threatening the belief of white privilege or, even worse, white supremacy gives promotion to the fear equation. What are you afraid of? Who gives you that much fear? It's a question that all who fall into that category should ask themselves.

In a report by Greg Howard of the Concourse, part of the reason we're seeing so many black men killed is that police officers are now best understood less as members of communities dedicated to keeping peace within them than they are as domestic soldiers. The drug war has long functioned as a full-employment act for arms dealers looking to sell every town and village in the country on the need for military-grade hardware, and 9/11 made things vastly worse with local police departments throughout America grabbing for cash to better defend against any and all terrorist threats. War had reached our shores, we were told, and police officers needed weaponry to fight it.

Officers have military-style tanks now. They have drones. They have automatic rifles and planes and helicopters and go through military-style boot camp training. It's a constant complaint from what remains of this country's civil liberty caucus. Just this last June, 2019, the ACLU issued a report on how police departments now possess arsenal which they couldn't wait to use. Few paid attention, as usually happens.

The worst part of outfitting our police officers as soldiers has been psychological. Give a man access to drones, tanks, and body armor, and he'll reasonably think that his job isn't simply to maintain peace but to eradicate danger. Instead of protecting and serving, police are searching and destroying. The whole idea of "shoot first, plant a weapon or drugs," is still too much a part of the insidious blue law where they protect their own at all cost.

How simple is it to say, "I killed him out of fear for my life," when you know the chances are that you will be found not guilty? Try having three to four black police officers kill a white person, and see if they get off.

Fear causes people to go to extraordinary things to get an advantage over their competitors. Consider words like *gerrymandering*. In the process of setting electoral districts, gerrymandering is a practice that attempts to establish a political advantage for a particular party or group by manipulating district boundaries to create partisan-advantaged districts. The resulting district apportionment is known as a gerrymander; however, that word can also refer to the process. Now consider another term–*gentrification*. Gentrification is a process of renovation of deteriorated urban neighborhoods by means of the influx of more affluent residents. This is a common and controversial topic in politics and in urban planning.

Gentrification can improve the quality of a neighborhood while also potentially forcing relocation of current established residents and businesses, causing them to move from a gentrified area, seeking lower-cost housing and stores. Gentrification often shifts a neighborhood's racial/ethnic composition and average household income by developing new, more expensive housing and businesses and improved resources. Conversations about gentrification have evolved as many in the social-scientific community have questioned the negative connotations associated with the word *gentrification*. One example is that gentrification can lead to community displacement for lower-income families in gentrifying neighborhoods as property values and rental costs rise; however, every neighborhood faces unique challenges, and reasons for displacement vary.

However, the correlation between the shortage of affordable housing and the subsequent displacement that results in gentrifying neighborhoods is not a debated fact. Displacement begins as landlords take advantage of rising market values and evict longtime residents in order to rent or sell to the more affluent. Some strategies to combat displacement include low-income, affordable housing and tighter housing regulations surrounding evictions. The source of this definition is Wikipedia. The political right particularly use these tactics to, in their minds, even the score on voting numbers because there are more Democrats in the country than Republicans.

Roughly estimated, there are 55 million registered Republicans, roughly 72 million Democrats, and roughly 42 million registered independents. The current population of the United States of America is approximately 327.16 million based on the latest United Nations estimates. There are a little over 30 million children under the age of eighteen (voting age), about 70 million adults over the age of eighteen (voting age), about 230 million adults registered to vote, about 170 million people who voted in the 2008 election: 122 million (a little over 2/3).

So you are beginning to get the picture. There is a lot to gain politically by the right if they stack the deck a bit and control some of these districts with heavy minority and women populations that, in large numbers, tend to vote Democratic.

CHAPTER 16

Tolerance

We must not only control the weapons that can kill us, we must bridge the great disparities of wealth and opportunity among the peoples of the world, the vast majority of whom live in poverty without hope, opportunity or choices in life. These conditions are a breeding ground for division that can cause a desperate people to resort to nuclear weapons as a last resort. Our only hope lies in the power of our love, generosity, tolerance and understanding and our commitment to making the world a better place for all.

–Muhammad Ali

THE WORD *TOLERANCE* means the ability or willingness to tolerate something, in particular the existence of opinions or behavior that one does not necessarily agree with. Because of the word *diversity*, which tends to make many uncomfortable, many merely tolerate those choosing to value it. If you are tolerating me, you are not valuing me. If you are not valuing me, then I become insignificant to your desires and wishes. You are listening to me but not truly hearing me. You see me but don't acknowledge me. You speak to me but fail to communicate with me.

Tolerance is defined, too, as "to bear or endure" or "to nourish, sustain, or preserve" or as "a fair, objective, and permissive attitude toward those whose opinions, beliefs, practices, racial or ethnic origins, etc. differ from one's own freedom from bigotry." Toleration may signify "no more than forbearance and the permission given by the adherents of a dominant religion for other religions to exist, even though the latter are looked on with disapproval as inferior, mistaken, or harmful." Actually, to tolerate me is to disrespect me. I would prefer direct honesty and candor even if it's of a negative nature versus a cloak of deception.

During the civil rights movement, cases such as *Plessy v. Ferguson* and *Brown v. Board of Education* forced the Jim Crow Southern states not to change their beliefs and ideals about race but to tolerate us. Unfortunately, history continues to repeat itself because it's no different today. The races simply tolerate one another versus really communicating and educating themselves about the things that they have had perceptions but very limited knowledge of. Perception becomes factual minus data to refute what is perceived.

If we get right down to it, we are much more similar than we are different. Our spring training may be quite different, but our primary seasons are quite similar. We were all conceived. We were educated to some degree. We eat with a fork, knife, and spoon. We drink from a container. We love pastimes like TV, travel, shopping, sports, entertainment. We work. We go to church. We forget key dates. We laugh. We cry. We love. We dislike—we . . . we . . . we . . .

Now where the problem rears its ugly head is in the degree to which we do these things and the atmosphere and persons who share in these experiences. We tend to gravitate toward those who think like us, agree with us, talk like us, etc. That is the point where the separation takes place and people start to take sides. People are not born hating one another; it's a learned behavior. Children will play with one another without any implicit bias until some alpha particle or gamma ray decides to invade the purity of their space.

Generations of hate are like a relay race; it is handed off from one person to another. The problem is that in passing the hate baton, the race never ends. It keeps circling the track through multigenerations. The only thing that changes darkness is light. The thing that will change the darkness of hate is the light of caring and love. We all are seeking life, liberty, and the pursuit of happiness per the Declaration of Independence. We are supposed to be endowed by our creators with certain inalienable rights, but are we all given those rights?

The attitudes of Jim Crow and the concept of "separate but equal" have its roots planted yesterday, but its limbs are reaching into today. There are still too many who believe that the races should be separate, that immigration is a cancer, that hate is a more valued behavior than love. Schools in many parts of the country even today remain separate and unequal. Though many of our inner-city young people are dependent on public education, the winds of change are bending toward charter schools. Though a more preferred form of education, can be a form of discrimination because many, particularly in the poorer parts of our nation, are not prepared for the criteria required to thrive in these fast-moving environments.

Are charter schools needed? For sure, if we are to catch up to the rest of the world in competence, but there has to be more of a strategic plan to get us from A to B and then C instead of jumping right to C. Every child does not learn at the same rate or have the same capabilities. Instead of focusing on the top of the scale, we should think about how to bring the middle and middle and bottom closer to the top.

To accomplish that daunting task, we as a nation need to place our focus on compensating teachers to a point where they want to remain in the system instead of jumping to other career fields in order to make them financially solvent. My sister, who passed away in 2007, was a teacher and professor in the school system for over twenty-five years. She was a highly skilled lecturer in speech and literature and spent over thirty-plus (30+) years in the profession. After laboring in the education vineyard for all those years, her salary was less than those she taught, who graduated and went into industries and services around the country.

Something is terribly wrong when the genesis of the teaching carries less importance than the eventual resulting product. These politicians run on a platform of bringing equity in pay to our teachers and professors, who labor in the vineyard to prepare our young minds for the world. Once in office, neither their efforts nor that of their union are able to reverse a trend that has gone on much too long of enslaving the compensation for our schoolteachers and professors.

CHAPTER 17

Implicit Bias

When it comes to meritocracy and diversity, the symbolic is real. And that means that simple actions that reduce bias, such as blind resume or application screening, are a double win: they reduce implicit bias and they help communicate our commitment to meritocracy.

–Eric Ries

AN IMPLICIT BIAS is the unconscious attribution of particular qualities to a member of a certain social group. Implicit bias is nothing more than a stereotypical categorization of a person or group. Implicit stereotypes are influenced by experience and are based on learned associations between various qualities and social categories, including race or gender.

When you make assumptions about an individual or group without facts and you base your actions and/or beliefs on those assumptions that could be wrong, then you bear shortchanging yourself as well as the individual or group. Some implicit bias about black people are "lazy," "always late," "broken family," "violent," "militant," "lack ambition," "inarticulate." I can find these characteristics in any class or culture, but the implicit bias is a developmental flat line for acceptance.

I experienced implicit bias while going to lunch with a CEO of a large corporation for which I was employed. As we approached the cafeteria area, the CEO couldn't help but notice that there was a table of blacks sitting near the entry. He commented, "Ted, why are all the blacks sitting together? Is there a problem? Why don't they integrate with the others around them? Do we have a diversity issue here that I am not aware of?"

As HR leader of the facility, it was my duty to not allow these comments to go unaddressed. I said, "It's strange that you see the one table of blacks sitting together but failed to see the other thirty or so tables of all whites sitting together. Why can't some of those at the thirty other tables join the blacks at their table? Why do you assume that there is a problem when one or more blacks are sitting together? Sometimes, people sit together because it's a matter of comfort and preference and not because there is an issue. We tend to sit where we are welcomed. The question is, How do we get the environment to a point where individuals are comfortable wherever they sit?"

This was not a time to kiss his ring or play politics. It was a time of teaching and not a time to be afraid to speak up on things that are part of my responsibility. Fortunately, the leader of that organization did have an open mind and was appreciative of my comments. In fact, it gave him a different perspective of looking at similar situations in the future. As a result of that conversation, diversity councils were established to address similar concerns in the future and advised HR and the site leadership on diverse issues. The CEO placed himself as a member of the council because he wanted to continually grow in his ability to deal with complicit bias. Sometimes, an individual gets one opportunity to make a change, and there is no time more impactful than the moment when the action or comment happens. Dr. Martin Luther King Jr. said in one of his speeches, "Noncooperation with evil is as much a moral obligation as is cooperation with good . . . To accept injustice or segregation passively is to say to the oppressor that his actions are morally right."

As people, we can't force anyone to see us or even include us, but we can demand respect. I would love for those who work with and for me to like me, but it's not necessary. What is necessary is that they respect me and that respect would be returned. In that same vein, if you fail to respect and get to know me, not include me, you have shortchanged both of us.

In another incident at that particular location in North Carolina, several individuals were sitting in a room with a view of the front of the building. It was a day when families were invited to the facility to see where their husbands and wives spend most of their days manufacturing gas turbines. As several of the adults casually continued their conversation, one of the white parents was incensed by two young boys wrestling on the grass outside the window (one white and one black).

Under stress, the true personality of a person can surface. The white male–who was visibly uneasy watching the kids aggressively challenge each other, assuming it was confrontational–rushed out to stop the kids from what he thought was a fight. As we continued to watch the kids play, it was obvious that it was boys just being boys and had nothing to do with the color of their skins. The white male was relieved to find that it was simply two kids playing. Sometimes, we adults let our personal biases infringe on our common sense. I wonder if both kids were white whether he would have been as quick to rush out to stop them or he would have had the same reaction. Even if the two were black, the reaction would have been different. We do have unconscious biases that creep into our normal reasoning process.

It is tough being black, brown, or different in America. I mentioned earlier in one of the chapters, if a white person is outspoken, he or she is considered aggressive; if a black person exhibits the same or similar behaviors, we are considered militant or hotheaded. If a white person is quiet, he or she is considered analytical, but the same behavior in blacks is called uninformed or nonparticipative. When whites are considered ambitious, we are considered impatient. These are but a few of the unconscious biases that exist toward people of differences. Is this the soul of America in decline?

CHAPTER 18

The Star-Spangled Banner

I've learned that people will forget what you said, people will forget what you did, but people will never forget how you made them feel.

--Maya Angelou

THE ARTICLE CITED by journalist Radley Balko quotes the rarely sung third stanza of the anthem (see below), noting that the phrase *hireling and slave* refers to black slaves hired to fight on the side of the British during the War of 1812:

> And where is that band who so vauntingly swore,
> That the havoc of war and the battle confusion
> A home and a country should leave us no more?

Their blood has wash'd out their foul footstep's pollution.

No refuge could save the hireling and slave
From the terror of flight or the gloom of the grave,
And the star-spangled banner in triumph doth wave
O'er the land of the free and the home of the brave.

There are historians (notably Robin Blackburn, author of *The Overthrow of Colonial Slavery, 1776–1848*, and Alan Taylor, author of "American Blacks in the War of 1812") who have indeed read the stanza as glorying in the Americans' defeat of the Corps of Colonial Marines, one of two units of black slaves recruited between 1808 and 1816 to fight for the British on the promise of gaining their freedom. Like so many of his compatriots, Francis Scott Key, the wealthy American lawyer who wrote "The Star-Spangled Banner," was a slaveholder who believed blacks to be "a distinct and inferior race of people, which all experience proves to be the greatest evil that afflicts a community."

We know pretty clearly that Key did not have the enslaved black population of America in mind when he wrote the words *land of the free*. It would be logical to assume as well that there may have been a degree of harboring resentment toward African Americans who fought for the British against the United States.

"With that in mind," writer Jon Schwarz on the website the Intercept, "think again about the next two lines, 'And the star-spangled banner in triumph doth wave / O'er the land of the free and the home of the brave.'"

The reality is that there were human beings fighting for freedom with incredible bravery during the war of 1812. However, "The Star Spangled Banner" glorifies America's "triumph" over them- and then turns that reality completely upside down, transforming their killers into the courageous freedom fighters.

After the United States and the British signed a peace treaty at the end of 1814, the United States government demanded the return of American "property," which by that point numbered about 6,000 people. The British refused. Most of the 600 eventually settled in Canada, with some going to Trinidad, where their descendants are still known as "Merikins."

In fairness, it has also been argued that Key may have intended the phrase as a reference to the British Navy's practice of impressment (kidnapping sailors and forcing them to fight in defense of the crown), or as a semi-metaphorical slap at the British invading force as a whole (which included a large number of mercenaries), though the latter line of thinking suggests an even stronger alternative theory – namely, that the word "hirelings" refers literally to mercenaries, and "slaves" refers literally to slaves.

It doesn't appear that Francis Scott Key ever specified what he meant by the phrase, nor does its context point to a single, definitive interpretation. I am sure that we will never know exactly what Key intended to convey, we can only assume from our perspective. I guarantee you that the explanations both for and against will be measured along racial lines....that I am sure.

Key originally wrote "The Star Spangled Banner" as a patriotic poem first published in a Baltimore newspaper shortly after the event that inspired it. Set to the tune of the popular English song "To Anacreon in Heaven," it became an unofficial national anthem during the 19th century, was officially adopted as such by executive order of President Woodrow Wilson in 1916, and confirmed by Congress as the national anthem of the United States in 1931. (David Emery, August 29, 2016)

Getting back to the Kaepernick issue of kneeling, why do we as a people—not race, not creed, not color—just allow the First Amendment to play itself out? Those who choose to stand, stand. Those who choose to kneel, kneel and let the games begin. Why do you, whoever you are, have to force me to do and feel as you do about a symbol, about an anthem that may or may not represent my people? No matter the reason, the First Amendment allows me to exercise my right to peacefully protest without being characterized as dishonoring the military, being un-American, or nonpatriotic. If you look around the stadium at any game, you will see individuals standing with their hats on, talking, walking, hands to their side, eating, etc. What makes this such a sour issue is that it plays into the racial divide in this country, and the bait-and-switch tactics of this president make matters worse. Consider excerpts from the black national anthem. How would those who are not black feel about standing and holding their hands over their hearts for this anthem:

"Lift Every Voice and Sing"

> (Verse 1)
> Lift every voice and sing, 'til earth and heaven ring,
> Ring with the harmonies of liberty;
> Stony the road we trod, bitter the chastening rod,
> Felt in the days when hope unborn had died;
> Yet with a steady beat, have not our weary feet
> Come to the place for which our fathers sighed?
>
> (Chorus 3)
> Shadowed beneath Thy hand, may we forever stand, True to our God, true to our native land.

Now really, would white people hold their hands over their hearts to honor this anthem? Without a doubt they would not because they would not and could not identify with the words. I rest my case.

According to BlackHistory.com, in 1939, renowned artist Augusta Savage received a commission from the World's Fair to create a sixteen-foot plaster sculpture, and she called it Lift Every Voice and Sing. With no funds to preserve the sculpture or cast it in bronze, the figure was destroyed by bulldozers at the close of the fair.

Throughout and following the civil rights movement, the song experienced a rebirth. By the 1970s, the anthem was often sung in succession with "The Star-Spangled Banner" at public events and performances across the United States at which there was a significant black population in attendance.

"Lift Every Voice and Sing" was entered into the Congressional Record as the official African American national hymn. I wonder how non–African Americans would feel about standing with their hands over their hearts for the anthem.

CHAPTER 19

The Importance of Education

The world is a book and those who do not travel read only one page.

--Augustine of Hippo

EDUCATION IS A tool that black America must use for social change to educate our youths and to correct the unconscious and conscious biases about the black community. No matter how you may feel about Bill Cosby, he spoke out against the parenting of inner-city youth a few years ago, and a firestorm erupted in the black community. Cosby argued that inner-city parents did not spend adequate time enforcing the importance of education in the black community.

Some called him elitist and out of touch, but in all honesty, he was correct in his assessment of the black community. Unfortunately, African Americans trail practically every other ethnic group across the country when it comes to standardized tests. The high school dropout rate for African American males is approximately 50 percent, and the incarceration rate for that group is approximately the same.

The year 2014 marks the fiftieth anniversary of *Brown v. Board of Education*, which theoretically ended school segregation in America. But many schools are as segregated today as they were before the ruling, and black children throughout the United States are performing at the bottom of the American educational system. The whole idea of magnet schools have brought on a new debate in the black community. Though magnet schools seem to be a cut above the public school system, some of our kids will be left behind because of the rigors of the magnet system. In the US education system, magnet schools are public schools with specialized courses or curricula. *Magnet* refers to how the schools draw students from across the normal boundaries defined by authorities as school zones that feed into certain schools.

The nation's capital, Washington, DC, in a state-by-state comparison, comes in last on reading exam. Seven percent of its black fourth-graders scored at or above proficient on the reading exam versus 70 percent of white fourth-graders. And while equal and adequate funding of our educational system is a major issue, it is not the only issue. For example, Prince George's County, Maryland, which is almost 70 percent black, is one of the most affluent black communities in the nation. Academically speaking, it's also one of the lowest-performing counties in Maryland.

An achievement gap gives way to an employability gap, an earnings gap, a health-care gap, a life expectancy gap, a housing gap, an incarceration gap, a marriage gap, a wealth gap, and other quality-of-life gaps. This achievement gap begins before children start school, widens between kindergarten and second grade, and is locked in by the third grade. The gap persists through elementary school, high school, college, and ultimately, the workforce. So we wonder why our black students have such a difficult time competing for fewer and fewer jobs. Well, stop wondering and help bridge the gap.

Without a quality education, many black children are being prepared for the streets, drug culture, violence, unemployment, prison, and death. Without a good education, black children will be unable to compete with the best and brightest students from all parts of the world for jobs in America. Without a good education, black children are not much better off than the slaves that they might be studying during Black History Month.

While the achievement gap is a difficult problem to solve, it is solvable. The key to fixing the problem is ensuring that black parents are active, invested, and involved in the educational lives of their children. Next, black children must be reinspired and motivated to do well in school. Many black students have simply turned away from education. Additionally, the funding, school resources, class size, teacher quality, and other factors needed to educate black children must be equal to that of other children. The parent-teacher connection that is directly related to improved student performance and high achievement must be strengthened. In addition, the black community must develop and maintain high academic standards for all black children—starting at birth.

The education of black children is not a priority in America. It must become one. The same national resolve that is necessary to wage war in Iraq and Afghanistan is needed to ensure that all children in America are well educated. While many individuals and institutions have a powerful role to play in reversing this problem, the black community must supply the leadership, energy, and resolve to fix it. The government must provide the financial resources and the legislative will. This issue must become a twenty-four-hours-a-day, 365-days-a-year national priority. The failure of black children to be educated in American schools is not their fault—adults are to blame. And it will take all Americans to fix this problem.

Education is the one thing that, once attained, can only be taken away when life has ended. No legislation, no police brutality, not even hate can take it away once it becomes your mantra. Education breeds confidence; it opens financial doors that are closed to many. It can bring the world to your doorstep through reading and traveling. You don't have to have acquired the title of genius, which is defined as receiving worldwide recognition or, as Socrates said, "hitting a target that no one else can even see." It's simply knowing your rights, understanding finance so that you are not totally dependent on others, understanding the laws that govern us, and applying your skill sets to accomplish your ultimate goal. It sounds pretty simple, but it's harder to accomplish because there are forces in the universe that are fixed in making the climb that much steeper.

How does all this relate to the subject matter of how this current administration views education primarily at the high school and college levels? Well, you received a full dose of reality with Trump's appointment of Betsy DeVos as secretary of education. DeVos is a former Republican Party chairwoman from Michigan and chair of the pro–school choice advocacy group American Federation for Children, and she has been proponent of the movement to privatize public education by working to create programs and pass laws that require the use of public funds to pay for private school tuition in the form of vouchers and similar programs. She has also been a force behind the spread of charter schools in Michigan, most of which have recorded student test scores in reading and math below the state average.

Don't get me wrong. Charter schools and private schools have proven to be a cut above the public school system. Its obvious personal bias plays a key role in what system they choose. Some equate private and charter schools' tuition with a superior education. Others are firmly committed to public schools because they provide a more diverse cultural experience. In my research, like traditional public schools, charter schools are free, and they can't discriminate against students because of their race, gender, or disability. However, parents must usually submit a separate application to enroll a child in a charter school, and like private schools, spaces are often limited.

Charter schools are independently run, and some are operated by for-profit private companies. On the other hand, most private schools depend on their own funding, which may come from parents through tuition, grants, donations, and endowments. Private schools also often actively seek money from alumni, businesses, and community organizations. If the school is associated with a religious group, as is the case with Catholic parochial schools, the religious organization–like the Catholic church–may be an important source of funding as well. Finally, in areas with a voucher system, some private schools are primarily funded by tuition paid for by a voucher from the state. Charter schools can also be hard to get into if they are popular, and they may use a lottery system to fill any vacancies.

Private schools are not required to accept every child and often require extensive applications that involve multiple interviews, essays, and testing. Private schools can be extremely selective: they can choose students based on not only their academic achievement but also their ethnicity, gender, and religion as well as the special resources of their parents.

One of the biggest concerns is that the education commission and Betsy DeVos are considering rolling back Obama administration guidance on school discipline that discouraged officers from disciplining students and pushed for more positive and less punitive responses to student behavior. In other words, the federal government will undo the Obama administration's work to keep students in school and out of the criminal justice system. The Department of Education is proposing to delay for two years an Obama era rule that requires states to aggressively address racial biases that may be channeling disproportionate numbers of minority children into special education.

It is a result of this type of information that I ask the question whether these private and charter schools are leaving many minority students behind. According to a recent Gallup poll, 78 percent of Americans believe that private schools provide a better education and prepare students for college at a greater rate than public schools. Charter schools are coming in at 60 percent, and traditional public schools, where the vast majority of K-12 students are educated, come in dead last, with only 37 percent of respondents expressing confidence in their merits.

CHAPTER 20

Trump Tax Hoax

We contend that for a nation to try to tax itself into prosperity is like a man standing in a bucket and trying to lift himself up by the handle.

—Winston Churchill

WE HAVE JUST recently received an overhaul of the tax process for all Americans. What does it mean to the majority of the middle- to lower-income taxpayers? Is it really tax relief for the lower part of the earning equation, or is it a windfall for the rich? According to author Kimberly Amadeo, the act keeps the seven income tax brackets but lowers tax rates. Employees will see changes reflecting in their withholding in their February 2019 paychecks. These rates revert to the 2017 rates in 2026. I encourage all my readers to really study this tax package because there are a lot of smoke and mirrors for those who are not wealthy.

We have billionaires running the country, so do you really believe that they will enact laws that will hurt themselves? These are oligarchs or, at least, aristocrats. Aristocracy is a government ruled by a few elite citizens. Does that, in any way, sound familiar? In Europe, the elite consisted of the nobility and higher clergy, often drawn from noble families. Usually, the elite positions in question are hereditary. It was one of the six forms of government identified by Aristotle, and he said it was the second best, after monarchy but before constitutional government. Moreover, if corrupted, it resulted in only the second worst form of government: oligarchy.

I encourage all my readers to get as much information as possible to understand how this upper-end tax primarily written for the rich will affect you and your families. Many large corporations confirmed they won't use the tax cuts to create jobs. Corporations are sitting on a record $2.3 trillion in cash reserves, double the level in 2001. The CEOs of Cisco, Pfizer, and Coca-Cola would instead use the extra cash to pay dividends to shareholders. The CEO of some companies will use the proceeds to buy back shares of stock. In effect, the corporate tax cuts will boost stock prices but won't create jobs.

The most significant tax cuts should go to the middle class who are more likely to spend every dollar they get. The wealthy use tax cuts to save or invest. It helps the stock market but doesn't drive demand. Once demand is there, then businesses create jobs to meet it. Middle-class tax cuts create more jobs. But the best unemployment solution is government spending to build infrastructure and directly create jobs.

The point here is, just don't take what the government tells you at face value. Check it out for yourself. Ask Mr. Trump how much he gained from this tax package. He won't tell you just like he won't reveal his taxes. Many in the world of work did not like drug testing because it infringed on their privacy. If you are not taking drugs, then what is the true concern? The same applies to the president's tax. What does he not want the general public to see? Is it that he is not as rich as he proclaims, that he is a poor employer to the many immigrants in his employ? Is it that he is truly a puppet to Russia and Putin? Is it that he does not understand the art of the deal? Whatever it is, our country made a tsunami of a mistake in allowing this individual to inhabit the White House.

(Data accumulated from a report written by Kimberly Amadeo in November of 2018 and Elena Holodny and Andy Kiersz in December of 2017.)

CHAPTER 21

Blind Loyalty

You're not supposed to be so blind with patriotism that you can't face reality. Wrong is wrong, no matter who says it.

—Malcolm X

THIS PRESIDENT, DONALD J. Trump, is changing the political and social landscape of America one legislation and one screwup at a time. Though this Congress is frustrated at his antics and his lack of leadership and poise, there is still blind loyalty. Blind loyalty means that someone has all faith in another person despite that person's shortcomings and faults. They will put their trust and faith in that individual and follow and support them against all odds. Blind in this sense means the person is ignorant or can't see the shortcomings or faults of the person they've put all their faith in.

Sarah Elizabeth Huckabee Sanders (born August 13, 1982) is an American campaign manager and political adviser who was appointed White House press secretary to President Donald Trump in July 2017. She places her credibility on the line every time she sets out to defend the policies, statements, and tweets of President Trump.

After Donald Trump was elected, Sanders was named to the position of deputy White House press secretary in his new administration. On May 5, 2017, she held her first White House press briefing, standing in for Press Secretary Sean Spicer, who was serving on Naval Reserve duty. On June 27, during a press briefing, Sanders, as was her custom, criticized the media, accusing them of spreading "fake news" against Trump. The *fake news* term was coined by Kellyanne Conway, an American pollster, political consultant, and pundit who is currently serving as counselor to the president in the administration of President Donald Trump. She was previously Trump's campaign manager, having been appointed in August 2016.

During her briefing, Sanders cited a video created by James O'Keefe. Although she was unsure of the video's accuracy, she said, "I would encourage everyone in this room and, frankly, everybody across the country to take a look at it." Without having the intricate details of the video, she plowed ahead to support something that she knew very little about. It's really a difficult place to be because she has to defend the position of the administration whether wrong or right. As a result, it has affected her credibility as a spokesperson.

Do we now have failed leadership in America? It's something to think about. We have a president who has divided the country along ethnic lines; a president who has no patience for details and refuses to sit through critical political and military briefings; a president who is more comfortable at Mar-a- Lago playing golf than he is in the Oval Office or with climate change, health care, or immigration; a president who involves himself in how he is perceived rather than what the country needs; and a president who interjected himself into the National Football League's kneeling incident without considering its origin.

Weekly, we observe Nazi and Confederate flags flying on our soil, but what this president chooses to comment on is a football player (black) who was not attempting to dishonor our veterans or the American flag but instead call attention to the disparate treatment that black and brown people are receiving at the hands of rogue segments of our police and justice departments across our country. This president, who made such an issue about kneeling during the national anthem, did not salute, as the other past presidents and their wives did, as the flag-draped coffin of our forty-second president, George H. W. Bush, passed during the funeral procession. There are several other occasions where this president during the national anthem stood with his hands to his side and not saluting. What a hypocrite!

Kneeling is a basic human position where one or both knees touch the ground. It can be used as an expression of reverence and submission. Reverence is "a feeling or attitude of deep respect tinged with awe; veneration." The word *reverence*, in the modern-day definition, is often used in relationship with religion. This is because religion often stimulates the emotion through recognition of God, the supernatural, and the ineffable. Reverence involves a humbling of the self in respectful recognition of something perceived to be greater than the self. Thus, religion is commonly a place where reverence is felt. Submission is the act of presenting a proposal, application, or other documents for consideration or judgment.

So what am I missing here, Mr. President? Where in all this does it refer to disrespect for the American flag or the national anthem, which in reality was not written with all American citizens in mind? This again is nothing more than red meat that you are throwing to your base. Most soldiers whom I have interviewed on the subject see nothing disrespectful about the silent and peaceful protest guaranteed to us by the First Amendment. In fact, we all fought to secure those rights, but you chose to make it a political football.

If many of our soldiers don't see this as a disrespect issue, then why do you, as one who has never served in a military sense, have the gumption to speak for us and throw shade on what the action of kneeling was really about? You chose to flip the script and protect the racist policemen and women who do not put on their uniform to protect and serve but instead to harass and intimidate.

Yes, Donald, you have forgotten or never knew that the government is not your sandbox to play with as you please. Though I truly believe that the man sitting in the Oval Office has never seriously cracked a book to read from cover to cover because his attention span is much too short, I truly wish he will visit the last paragraph of the Gettysburg Address, which states, "It is for us, the living, rather to be dedicated here to the unfinished work which they have, thus far, so nobly carried on. It is rather for us to be here dedicated to the great task remaining before us that from these honored dead we take increased devotion to that cause for which they gave the last full measure of devotion that we here highly resolve that these dead shall not have died in vain; that this nation shall have a new birth of freedom; and that this government of the people, by the people, for the people, shall not perish from the earth."

The owners in the National Football League who hold our president up in his obvious wrongs are those who see the theme "Make America Great Again" as their anthem. They have created a million-dollar plantation, and the laws on that plantation are the Jim Crow laws of old. They take literally their title as owners, and they move the chattel around as they please. They use the excuse of not wanting to upset the president when, in reality, they have yearned to reconstruct the old plantation mentality for years.

Take a look around at the next sports event that you attend. There are people talking, walking, texting, taking pictures with their phones, etc. What constitutes disrespect in the eyes of those who are so objective to kneeling? People have burned the flag, wrapped it around themselves like a blanket, and wore it as a piece of garment, but a black man kneeling has this effect?

Laura Ingraham's comment on Fox News to LeBron James to stay in his place, stay out of politics, and "shut up and dribble" is a part of the plantation mentality, and the tragedy in this is they feel it's okay because "they are not racist." Here again is another case of implied bias. She went to great lengths to invite LeBron to her show as if to say no hard feelings. She went on to defend herself by saying that she had said similar things for over fifteen years. All that says to me is, you have had hatred and bigotry in your heart for twice that long based on your age. White privilege or not, you don't get to say what you want and not expect blowback.

CHAPTER 22

The International and Domestic Perspective on Trump

What kind of times are these–this is not somewhere else but here, our country moving closer to its own truth and dread.
–Adrienne Rich

T HE FACT IS, we now live in a global economy that is easily affected by current values/changes, political decisions, climate changes, and governmental structures. Recent actions by our president related to immigration, tariffs, historical agreements, and relationship with our allies have proven how tied we are to countries and cultures around the globe.

In order to get a current perspective of what effect this current administration is having not only on the domestic policies, treaties, tariffs, etc. but also on the global economy, I have interviewed a few people from other parts of the world. I wanted the perspective of those outside the boundaries of President Trump's purview to give their unvarnished opinion of our situation here in this country. I reached out to a few resources in the international space to get their opinions on not just the man Trump but also the effects he and his policies are having on the country's economic index.

One such resource was Fabio Cadeddu. Mr. Cadeddu is an Italian lawyer trained in prestigious American and English law firms and was admitted to the Italian bar in 2004. He advises clients on international trade, shipping ports and terminals. He is a member of the International Propeller Club of Naples and is admitted before the Italian supreme court.

In questioning Mr. Cadeddu, I was interested in his position on our current leadership climate as well as how the current policy affects the culture and political satire. The use of the term *satire* is appropriate in my view because it is the use of humor, irony, exaggeration, or ridicule to expose and criticize people's stupidity or vices, particularly in the context of contemporary politics and other topical issues. You have to say that President Trump resembles those descriptive based on his erratic, misguided, and racist–yes, I said it, racist–leadership during the first quarter of his administration.

According to Mr. Cadeddu, "The political climate in America is out of control and this president even confuses himself. From my perspective, he can't seem to remember what he said from one minute to another. He contradicts himself constantly. He seems detached from reality and seems to lack the educational gene necessary to do the job that has a trickle-down effect on world markets. I am not sure President Trump knows where North Korea is without someone telling him, and it was obvious that he didn't understand the political climates or the potential downside to negotiating with either China or North Korea. There was not an ounce of possibility that Kim Jung Un would negotiate anything without China's approval. Kim Jung Un played him like a fiddle, and so did Xi Jinping, president of China. I ask you, Ted, has any positives come as a result of his so-called summit in South Korea? The answer has to be *no* and a resounding *no* because Kim Jung Un would be foolish to give up his nukes, which is his, no pun intended, 'Trump card' in future negotiations."

He continued, "There is a serious concern on the part of the international communities, as a whole. Because of his erratic behavior and failure to understand the specifics and details of world politics, he could be a danger to your country and the world. It was his observation that Trump seems to surround himself with loyalist whether they were qualified or not." I must agree with Fabio—this is nepotism and cronyism at its finest.

It was obvious to Mr. Cadeddu that President Trump values loyalty over competence as in the case of many who now have left his administration because either they realized the mistake they had made or they were improperly selected and placed in positions that they were ill prepared for. Because of the need for skilled, savvy politicians who have labored in the trenches and see the need and value in working across political lines, incompetence will, sooner or later, be exposed as in many of the cases of those leaving the administration. "If the people of the United States fail to see President Trump's own incompetence and lack of political substance as the leader of the free world, the United States could lose it standing on the world stage," said Fabio.

Mr. Cadeddu continued his comments by drawing a comparison of President Trump to President Silvio Berlusconi, an Italian media tycoon and politician who served as prime minister of Italy in four governments. In 2018, *Forbes* magazine ranked him as the 190th richest man in the world with a net worth of $8 billion. Forbes also ranked him twelfth in the list of "The World's Most Powerful People" due to his domination of Italian politics throughout more than twenty years (20) as the head of the center-right coalition. In his opinion, the difference between the two was that Berlusconi was definitely a power broker, but he was not stupid.

Berlusconi was prime minister for nine (9) years in total, making him the longest-serving postwar prime minister of Italy and the third longest-serving since Italian unification, after Benito Mussolini and Giovanni Giolitti. He is known for his populist political style and brash, overbearing personality. Who does that remind you of? In his longtime tenure, he was often accused of being an authoritarian leader and strongman. On August 1, 2013, he was convicted of tax fraud by the Supreme Court of Cassation (Wikipedia). Are you beginning to see why Fabio has compared these two and their leadership styles?

"I don't know how he considers himself a good businessman when he is afraid to share with the American people his plan to protect the American economy," says Fabio. "The man does not respect the environment, nor does he understand the long-term effect of climate change. The stupidity of a person to not recognize that climate change is a universal and global issue and the wind and oceans carry pollution in all directions and to all parts of the world. There is pollution from cars, planes, trains, buses, and fuels.

"There are plastics being tossed in our waterways, intense storms that are more severe than in the past, ice caps melting, etc., and with these happening, there are still debates inside his administration on whether climate change is a real issue. I am not sure that he knows or even cares." What about tariffs on the economy, I asked. His response was that tariffs have a trickle-down effect. They directly affect one country's economy, which then affect another country's economy as it is with China and the United States, two of the world's largest importers and exporters now battling a tariff war.

The final question for Fabio related to how the media reacts to the idea coined by Trump of *fake news*. His opinion is that the Italian media could be very critical at times but, in aggregate, was fairly neutral on political matters. He believes that the Italian media, as a whole, has tried to be fair to Trump but is quite open about the fact of this president having a problem telling the truth. He changes his position in an instant. "Our media, as most of our citizens are, seems focused on his self-aggrandizing ways with less emphasis on the needs of the country. I hope that now the people of the United States are starting to realize what a grave mistake they made in electing what I and others consider to have been a terrible choice. People in Italy are free to speak openly about their feelings on President Trump and believe it. There is very little support in our country for this man. These and other comments have weakened the brand of the United States in the world market."

The ability to solve world problems of climate change, tariffs, human relations, civil disorder, immigration, sharing of the world's resources, and political differences will be rooted not in our military might but instead in our ability to negotiate and use capable intellectual capital from the global community. The country is more divided than any time in recent history because of this president's rhetoric. This divisive rhetoric has often led to civil disorder and loss of life.

These current events and decisions on the part of this administration have exposed the underbelly of the country, and what is exposed is simply weakening our influence globally. Whoever is successful in unseating this demagogue will have an uphill battle to repair the cracks in the world's infrastructure brought on by this regressive leader. The word for this president is simply *un-American.*

It's not the size of your hands, your crying fake news, your bank account, or even your access to power but instead the size of your heart and the ability to unite the country and rally others around your ideas. This president seems incapable of being a collaborator other than with our competitors.

In an attempt to get more of the international perspective, a similar question was asked of a friend and business colleague from England (unnamed). Being an astute political enthusiast, he is always willing to share his perspective of leadership gone wild here in America. Those who have always looked up to the US global leadership have had to pump the brakes and reassess how such a powerful country could have made the mistake of hiring what seems to be a puppet to the dictators of the world. Below is his answers to my questions on this administration.

1. What do you think of the current US president and his first year in office?

During the presidential campaign, Donald Trump pledged to "drain the swamp" and clear Washington of lobbyists. During the US president's first year in office, the opposite proved true. In addition to Michael Cohen (President Trump's personal lawyer and longtime fixer) being sentenced to three years in prison on fraud and lying charges and Paul Manafort (the former Trump campaign chairman) being found guilty on eight federal counts of bank and tax fraud and pleading guilty to one count of conspiracy to obstruct justice and one count of conspiracy against the US, thirty-two others have been charged so far as a result of the special counsel's investigation. This is a clear breach of one of the fundamental campaign promises.

The various investigations surrounding the president have distracted the business of government and diverted untold hours away from valuable matters. But rather than admit any possibility of wrongdoing, the president screams witch hunt and attacks anyone whom he deems as not being blindly and unendingly loyal to him personally.

Another of the key promises candidate Trump made was to build the wall and make Mexico pay. President Trump failed to deliver on this pledge in his first year. And far from making Mexico pay, President Trump gloated that he is "proud to shut down the government" and took the mantle for the Trump shutdown that led to eight hundred thousand federal employees going without pay. The comment by President Trump, "If we don't get what we want one way or the other, I will shut down the government" and storming out of meetings with Democrats regarding that point were characterized by Senate minority leader Chuck Schumer as a temper tantrum.

The president's approach to the shutdown is characteristic of his approach in general–Machiavellian. In his mind, the ends seem to justify the means, whatever they are. It is a "win at all costs" approach that is intentionally aggressive by nature. Whether it be name-calling or the use of vulgar language, President Trump's demeanor and personality, perhaps more than any of his policies, have debased the Office of the President.

2. Were you surprised that he was elected? If so why?

Yes and no. Yes, that someone who has been so vulgar in his behavior and discourse could reach the highest position in American politics. No, because the Democrats fielded Hillary Clinton, whose family scandals are well-documented and who is an extremely polarizing figure. So the fact that many in the US were reviled by the prospect of her presidency and a Clinton "dynasty," translating into poor electoral performance was not surprising.

3. How is the US viewed in your country under this new leader?

The country is viewed as painfully divided and led by someone with limited logical and emotional intelligence.

4. Has tariffs affected your country in any way? If so, how?

Yes. The US decision to impose a 25 percent tax on steel and a 10 percent tax on aluminum from the EU has affected the UK. According to UK Steel, the body that represents steel producers across the country, 7 percent of steel exports go to the US, worth £360 million. These tariffs were characterized by the UK trade secretary as "disappointing" and "absurd."

Tariffs and the threat of tariffs can be used as a negotiation stick. Doing business with the US or not doing business with the US can have a vital effect on an economy. For example, post-Brexit, the UK could bow to pressure from the US to allow hormone-reared beef into the UK market, despite proven carcinogenic risks. Clearly, lowering health and safety standards for food products would have profound effects.

5. Our president doesn't believe that many of the world's major disasters are related to climate change. What do you think?

President Trump doesn't believe in climate change. He has said, "The concept of global warming was created by and for the Chinese in order to make US manufacturing noncompetitive." So his position that major disasters are not related to climate change doesn't surprise me. I believe he is wrong and that we need to find the "cleanest" ways to live and for the need to develop sustainable energy in order to reduce the environmental effects we have on our planet both for moral and practical reasons.

6. Do you have an opinion of the two-party system in the United States?

Not at this time.

7. Why do you think is President Trump so closely tied to Putin?

After a nearly two-year investigation, the Mueller report cleared President Trump of collusion with the Russians to influence the 2016 election. But it did not clear the president of obstruction of justice. People in the president's inner circle did things they should not have and lied about it as evidenced by the indictments for thirty-four individuals, seven of whom have been convicted so far. The reasons for the lies have yet to come out. But the FBI investigation into whether President Trump was working for Russia while in office indicates a concern that President Trump is an agent of Vladimir Putin. While that sounds like a conspiracy theory, it is very difficult to come away with many other reason(s) to explain why President Trump has been so friendly with the president of Russia and chooses to align himself with and has gone on record as supporting President Putin more so than his own intelligence and security forces.

Another perspective of this administration was shared by a young lady whom I highly respect. I wanted to get not only the international perspective but also how a different gender viewed this political climate, knowing how Trump has disparaged women before and after his assuming office. The questions are as follows:

1. What do you think of the current US president and his first year in office?

It is horrifying. My high school history teacher once told our class that one of the most important reasons for studying history is to not repeat its mistakes–apparently, that lesson has not resonated with the American people. The bar for acceptable behavior is set lower each day. Everything from human rights to the environment is under attack. I don't know where to donate or what to support because there are too many causes in jeopardy. I am writing this while listening to Michael Cohen's testimony outlining Trump's blatant corruption, the corruption of one of the most powerful figures in the world. What is even more surprising is that Trump seems to operate without accountability to the very people who got him elected, and it is forgiven even when his supporters are the ones most negatively impacted by his decisions. Case in point is his promise to bring manufacturing jobs back to the United States with the Carrier Corporation in Indiana. To use an appropriately colloquial term, it was a dog-and-pony show with no real benefit to the workers in the end. I think it is a willful ignorance or naivety that allows him to operate without culpability and continue to infringe on our democratic system.

2. Were you surprised that he was elected? If so, why?

Absolutely. I remember calling my brother as the election results came in and asking, "Is this really happening?" He had no response. He tried to say that it couldn't be real and we still had time. Unfortunately, there were a lot of unforeseen factors that came into play with an election in an era of social media. Media helps win elections and maintain powers—it is the dissemination of information, the control of information, the manipulation of information. How people choose and are able to listen, watch, and learn strengthens whatever narrative they believe.

How could a time of such hope with Obama turn into a reality TV star winning the US presidency? I understand history is cyclical in this way, but does it have to be so extreme? I was surprised when we elected a black man but more surprised we could elect a man who is the antithesis of the progress we seemingly made. In retrospect, it is not all that surprising when I consider there is an America outside of the liberal bubble I have always comfortably lived in, but I still had hope for the future that is now fleeting.

3. How is the US viewed in your country under this new leader?

As the laughingstock of the world and unfortunately setting the tone for international elections. It has emboldened behavior and political parties that have previously been the minority. Now I want to consider this minority to be the loudest one heard, bullying their way into power in every sense of the word.

4. Has tariffs affected your country in any way? If so, how?

I am not close enough to the situation to have been versed on the particulars related to tariffs, so I will pass on this question.

5. Our president doesn't believe that many of the world's major disasters are related to climate change. What do you think?

I am not sure he actually believes in many of the things he says. When someone is such a compulsive liar, it is hard to parse any truth from their words. So much of what he promotes is tainted by his need to further a self-serving agenda. I am sure if it suited his personal wealth, he would believe in climate change; but right now, he will "believe" whatever is most profitable. Ignorance is bliss if you can temporarily buy that ignorance and never be confronted by the consequences of your actions.

6. Do you have an opinion of the two-party system in the United States?

It is highly problematic and not representative of the diverse population of the United States. It creates an imbalanced government, replacing it with a black-and-white system with very little room for compromise. Furthermore, the structure is so ingrained in our minds as the only option available we don't even allow a fair opportunity for other parties to be considered. Instead, the "other" party is seen as the reason for an opposing party's success, leeching votes from the candidate who comfortably fits within the two existing parties.

7. Why do you think is President Trump so closely tied to Putin?

It is a power play that we will probably never really know the root of. If I were to consider the dynamics from a historical perspective of countries wielding power through political manipulation, I would say perhaps it's a shift in American imperialistic strength. If we were once the ones putting political allies in power in foreign countries, maybe the same is now happening to us in a transfer of world power.

Another opinion of the current administration was shared by Professor James Simpson. Professor Simpson currently serves as adjunct lecturer in finance at Bronx Community College of the City University of New York. He is a part of the business and information systems department. His work experience includes but is not limited to providing comprehensive financial modeling studies used in capital structure analysis for internal determination of credit worthiness and as supportive submission when seeking formal public ratings from the agencies. Professor Simpson, in addition to his other duties, also serves as chairman of trustees at Hyde Leadership Charter School in New York. Below are the questions Professor Simpson was asked to elaborate on:

1. What do you think of the current US president and his first year in office?

I am not a fan of the US president on a number of levels. On a nonemotional level, I do not think that he has provided intelligent or effective leadership to the country on any matters that lead to the general well-being. Save for the lowering of corporate taxes (which I supported), his actions on just about every other matter have been left-footed, myopic, without a strategic perspective, and wholly self-serving. His caustic disposition has aggravated the country's long-term allies and given hope to our long-term competitors and enemies. His actions have tarnished our position as the leading global power in almost every measure. But for the fact that the US system of national governance divides power and authority, we could see such a president attempt to place himself in autocratic control of the nation much like we've seen in South America and Africa. I am not supportive of the strongman, autocratic, nationalistic leader. I am in favor of trade and open correspondence. This president seems to believe we are a nation of peasants. I will certainly work to defeat this president at the next general election.

2. Were you surprised that he was elected? If so, why?

I was very surprised that this president was elected. I had no idea that the inhabitants of the Rust Belt states were so bad off that they would follow and support a snake oil salesman such as the president. Equally, I had no idea that so many of the US voting public held such a dim view of Clinton. I also was not watching to notice that the Dems were running such a poor race for the White House. I thought that the bombast brought to the primary competition by the soon-to-be president would be fully discounted as the noise of a joker and pretender. I had no inkling that Middle America was lead amuck to such a degree and would follow such a pied piper. I also underestimated the resilience of racism throughout the land. But such bigotry goes hand in hand with the anxieties the underemployed Rust Belters have been suffering for some time. Again, on a current basis, I was just not aware.

3. How is the US viewed in your country under this new leader?

As a US citizen, I can say that I fear other nations fear that the US will/is being viewed as having lost its course. It is not the leader of nations with a lofty vision of what could be the betterment for all its people. I fear that the birth defect of the nation is being viewed more openly and obviously than it has since the 1960s.

4. Has tariffs affected your country in any way? If so, how?

I, as a US citizen, do suffer from the tariffs because it directly eliminates products I want to use or makes them terribly expensive. This is theoretical for the moment but could certainly be my personal case. I have no information that any of the tariff tampering has done any good thing for the US employee. I do know that these maneuvers have weakened the US relationship with our trading partners and foes alike. I can argue that the intent may have been correct, but the execution was disastrous.

5. Our president doesn't believe that many of the world's major disasters are related to climate change. What do you think?

I think the president is a dunce. Only an idiot would rebuke the majority opinion of scientists.

6. Do you have an opinion of the two-party system in the United States?

Having lived under a parliamentary system of national government for a number of years, ever since my return, I have complained that the US two-party system is inefficient and not truly representative. This is exacerbated by the existence of the Electoral College and also by the ability of the party in power to gerrymander to retain ballot power. In essence, the system is not representative, not truly fair.

7. Why do you think President Trump is so closely tied to Putin?

I think President Trump has some personal business dealings that enjoins Putin in some way. I also think his ego forces him to be attracted to manly men who wield authoritarian power.

Of course, all of this hoopla could just be a bad dream, or maybe the president is some sort of CIA superoperative and his behavior and manifest ethics are just some dance choreographed by the CIA on the global stage to aid the US in gaining advantage against all others. They say life is stranger than fiction!

Another educator at a major university took the time to share his assessment of the current political climate. It is a special treat to get the prospective of an administrator from the standpoint of his having access to four (4) generations of opinions. Those four generations are the generation X, the millennials, generation Z, as well as the baby boomers, who are primarily in administrative positions in educational facilities all over the country. Below is his perspective:

1. What do you think of the current US president and his first year in office?

President Trump has had a disastrous first two years of presidency perhaps of any in history. Not only has he failed to fulfill most of his promises—e.g., build the wall with Mexico and make them pay for it, draining the swamp, etc.–but he was also able to get Congress to pass his "greatest tax reform plan in history." The latter was clearly designed to benefit the top 1 percenters and big businesses but does little or nothing for small businesses and the rest of the country. Unfortunately, he also has appointed mostly unqualified and inexperienced people to his cabinet and to leadership positions in most government departments, with the primary criteria for appointment being that they are loyal to him. From his first day in office to the present, we have seen evidence of the extent of his narcissism and sociopathy, his willingness to say whatever comes to mind, no respect for the truth or the law, and the willingness to do whatever is necessary to meet his needs regardless of the consequences.

This White House is probably the most hate-oriented, disorganized, and incompetent environment that I am familiar with in recent decades, with many of the members of his organization appearing to be incompetent. Unfortunately, the Republicans in Congress also appear to be incapable of fulfilling their responsibilities to hold the executive branch accountable as a coequal branch of government. Because of the incompetence of Trump and his administration and the impotence of Congress, the country is facing a major constitutional crisis.

2. Were you surprised that he was elected? If so, why?

Yes, I could not imagine that someone so vulgar, disrespectful, and uncouth would not be chosen to be president, especially to replace Obama. However, in retrospect, low- and working-class whites and white nationalists who are economically and politically marginalized were politically awakened and saw their opportunity to have a candidate who would reverse many of the Obama's legacy and to gain preferential treatment. We also underestimated the anger against Hillary Clinton and the mistakes that she would make in her campaign, as well as the failure of many citizens of color to go to the polls and support a progressive social agenda. However, I suspect that many who voted for him are now distressed by his behavior, dishonesty, and lack of qualification for the presidency, and we will have the opportunity to correct this mistake in 2020.

3. How is the US viewed in your country under this new leader?

The US, since Trump, has lost the confidence and respect of the rest of the world. Most foreign leaders are concerned about the reversal of foreign policy toward a more nationalistic, US-first foreign policy and the unpredictability and ignorance of Trump especially with respect to foreign policy. The US will have a lot of corrective work with allies once Trump is out of office, and that will take a long time and considerable effort by those who replace him.

4. Has tariffs affected your country in any way? If so, how?

As far as I know, my home country has not been directly targeted by tariffs. That said, however, the US's role and influence in Panama has been significantly reduced, with China making significant inroads into the country with strategic investments in Panamanian infrastructure, including investing in the upgrade and widening of the Panama Canal.

5. Our president doesn't believe that many of the world's major disasters are related to climate change. What do you think?

There is little doubt from the current scientific evidence that global warming is a major threat to the health of the planet. In fact, recent evidence indicated that the global weather problems appear to be accelerating, and as such, we are getting closer to the tipping point from which the earth may not recover. The clock is ticking, and we need to replace Trump as quickly as possible and become more aggressive in developing and implementing a comprehensive environmental repair worldwide set of policies.

6. Do you have an opinion of the two-party system in the United States?

American democracy is a complicated system that is messy and vulnerable to malfunction, in part because of the corrupting role of big money and greed in government. While the two-party system can work effectively, recent divisiveness in Congress and the investment in ideology rather than in the principles on which this country was built have created a crisis that will take considerable time and effort to repair.

7. Why do you think is President Trump so closely tied to Putin?

The evidence is clear that the Russians were actively involved in trying to influence the 2016 elections in Trump's favor. What is also clear is that Trump admires and looks up to Putin and similar authoritarian leaders. That said, however, the question of whether Trump is allied with Putin directly remains to be demonstrated. Even if there is no formal demonstrable link to Putin and to Russian millionaires, it is clear that Trump is incapable for dealing effectively with the threat that Putin and Russia poses to the US.

The following and final answers to these questions come from someone truly special to me as a friend, someone in the financial field and whom I am confident is well versed on world issues well beyond his years. There are but a few true friends who cross your path in a lifetime, and this young man definitely made a major impression in my life as well as the lives of others whom he has befriended. His wisdom, candor, and fearless opinions are only surpassed by his integrity and superior intellect. Below are his answers to the same questions:

1. What do you think of the current US president and his few years in office?

I have to say that I am very surprised that Donald Trump was elected as president of the United States. I do not believe that he has the necessary skills to run a big and powerful country like the United States of America. It is still a mystery to me as to why US citizens would vote for change. An unnecessary change of a change, I would call it. We worked so hard for years to try to accomplish the most advanced and powerful country in the world. But the most important thing in my opinion is also to maintain the balance of what we have achieved, a balance that is necessary for all of us as a society.

I would very strongly suggest to every US citizen to *please* do the homework and understand that every short-term change or decision-making will heavily impact the long-term future of generations to come. I highly recommend that we, the US citizens, can look around the world and understand how appreciative we should be to America, the land of the opportunities that no other country has. Yes, I said it right. *No* other country.

I have traveled to more than fifty countries, and I don't believe or think that any country can represent opportunities like United States. That is why it is crucial for us to understand what kind of change we are looking for. The routine and monotony are part of the balance.

We have to remind ourselves all the time that everything we invest or consume today will impact our future.

I have been in the US since the presidency of George W. Bush and Barack Obama eras, and for the first time ever, I am shocked at who the country has decided to elect as a president of the US. The only comment I find for him is OPUD (overpromise and underdelivery). It does sound harsh, but that is the truth. In fact, I do not blame the president for trying to achieve any of the promises because they are simply unrealistic and impossible to accomplish. "I will create more jobs than God has ever created," Trump said during his campaign. Even a child anywhere in the world and not just in the US would understand that this is the most absurd thing someone would ever say or promise.

I understand that during a campaign, you could do and promise many things to lure and attract people to vote for you, but this is a different reality—a reality that perhaps even in Trump's mind is so abstract that he is even more confused than the rest of us combined in trying to understand what he is seeking to accomplish.

After the bizarre and unrealistic promises during a campaign that he shockingly won, he continues, as president, to promise things that are very obvious and nonrealistic. There is no particular science to explain any of the promises, but it is called arithmetic, and the numbers do not make sense. It is really nice to have lower taxes and other benefits that the president offers, but without productivity, unfortunately, these will come back to us at some point. What we are doing today is borrowing from our future growth with the hope that we do achieve the growth and pay it back. That sounds very nice if in fact we do create productivity and growth, but without balance and financial stability, the equation and the economic mechanism will most likely fail.

I am also very surprised how this president has approached the international politics that has affected many countries through tariffs. I am supportive that we should play the best politics that helps the United States first, but not to the point that can hurt severely other countries. If we continue to do that, at some point, it will affect us in the form of higher prices of goods and services. Many countries are directly and indirectly impacted from the tactics that Trump is imposing and proposing. I am hopeful that one day, he will understand that most of the countries are connected in many ways, and when one country is impacted by tariffs, it will then indirectly impact other countries that are directly doing business with that country. That's why, again, balance is absolutely the key to victory.

It is fascinating to me that someone born and raised in America like Trump doesn't seem to get the seriousness of climate change. It is scientifically proven that this phenomenon is imperative, and companies throughout the world have been investing for years now billions of dollars as it is seriously becoming a global threat. Yet our stubborn, high-tempered president refuses to understand why the rest of the world is urgently trying to make the best they can to avoid major disasters as a result of climate changes. Worse than that, even if we refuse to believe in climate change, we are actually experiencing that ourselves—oceans are rising at an alarming rate, wildfires are more intense, storms are more violent, floods are happening more frequently, and tsunamis are devastating cultures around the world. It is no longer safe to say that we fully experience the four seasons in our country. It is statistically proven that more and more people are getting ill as a result of climate changes. Yet and ironically, we have a president who says, "Nobody understands climate change better than me."

But things also get out of control when you have Russia or, in particular, Putin having an influence not only in Brexit and other global changes but now also to the election of the United States. Our Mr. Puppet President, as many would call him, instead of using his energy to fight everyone against and around him, should seriously reflect and compromise for the purpose of letting this country thrive (like it used to) for many of the years to come. There is a reason why Russia has and will continue to have a dictator that goes from president to prime minister and back and forth to keep controlling everything. We have publicly recognized 137 new billionaires from Russia who have created their wealth through Putin's regime. It is obvious that almost all the Russian citizens, including friends that I know, have ever expressed any support for their current president. But we are the United States, and this is our democracy.

We recognize well the separation of power, and we have no tolerance or room for noncooperative, high-tempered leaders. It has never worked, and it will always fail. For those of you who do not agree, I can respectfully ask you to go back and study the world history for the past one hundred years. No country has survived through dictatorship (China, Japan, Italy, Germany), and that's what we are indirectly facing. We have a racist, undeserving leader who is so unfit in any way, shape, or form to consider himself the leader of this country. God bless America, and I am hoping that this interview will inspire and encourage many young people like myself to carefully invest in our future. I say to you, young people, "If you don't like what you see, don't just sit back and watch. Get involved in politics, science, math, engineering, finance, investment, and other careers that will assist in changing the future for all of us.

MY FINAL THOUGHTS

WE NOW NAVIGATE this new reality and new norms where storms are more violent, ice caps are melting at an alarming rate, racial and radical hate groups are on the rise, cheating scandals at our major universities take headlines, there is little confidence in our leadership on the world stage, brown and black countries are targeted as shithole countries, women who are the mothers of a nation are disrespected, immigrants are refused entry unless they come from predominately white borders, and admiration is shown to those leaders from Russia, China, and North Korea, who would love to see our nation in ashes.

This president who threatens schools to not release his academic records, cozies up to dictators, embraces white nationalists, embarrasses himself on the national stage, attacks anyone other than his followers, is totally clueless of what *Brexit* means, and literally refuses to take briefings from the Justice Department—this is the quality of person at the helm of the most powerful country in the world. How absolutely scary is that?

Knowing this troubling data, it is abundantly clear to me, if not to you, that the central figure in all the negative karma is none other than the leader of the most powerful nation in the world, our president, Donald J. Trump. Columnist and political commentator George Will summed it up with two words: this president is *pathologically insecure*, and this is what we can expect for the length of his presidency.

Before you vote in the next election, consider what you have seen thus far in his administration. Those who continue to support him are saying to themselves that he is living to his promises. Well, is he? Do we have a wall between the United States and Mexico that Mexico is paying for? If there ever is a wall, you can bet that the American taxpayers will foot the bill. Are you better off under this new tax plan? You may have a few more dollars in your pocket in the first year, but watch what happens to your taxes in the other years. Has he brought jobs back to this country as promised? Absolutely not. These corporations will manufacture products where they can maximize the bottom line for their stockholders. Name one large company that has moved major portions of their operations back to the United States.

The economy is much better not because of him but because of eight years of preparation and sacrifice by the prior administration under President Obama. He is the beneficiary of some tough bipartisan decision of the prior administration. I do give Trump credit for continuing on a positive track on the major economic indicators, such as job creation, the stock market, and unemployment.

What happens if he eliminates, as he is trying to do, Obamacare, or the Affordable Care Act? Many of you who voted for him will be without medical coverage. What happens to the promise that he would spend more time in the White House than Obama and less time on the golf course? What happened to draining the swamp? The swamp is running over with slimy, slithering Polly-gators, even more than there were before. All of you who voted for this man were led astray, ran amuck, bamboozled, hoodwinked, and bedazzled by his celebrity. Now you know! Please don't repeat this catastrophe in 2020.

Before you pull the lever in 2020, consider these facts:

1. Trump is attempting to strip Medicare from more than one hundred thousand low-income people in some states.
2. He protects Confederate monuments, which are stains on the history of our great country. You may say, as he does, that these monuments are simply historic reminders of the past; but for black and brown people, it's a reminder of how hateful and racist the country was then and, to a degree, still is.
3. Think about his policy in separating children from their families at the border and placing them in cages.

4. Voting rights are under attack across this great country to continually weaken our democracy. Gerrymandering and ID laws are attempting to disrupt the democratic process and sway the pendulum in one direction. These actions are being undertaken by the political right to attempt to gain an advantage, knowing that the numbers are not in their favor.

5. There has been little to no action toward revamping gun laws in this country even after many of our schoolchildren have been slaughtered in schools, which should be safe zones. This president is a major supporter of the NRA, which, in my mind, is preventing true progress from being made on gun control.

6. Building a border wall has become more of an obsession with this president versus a necessity for immigration control.

7. Lying has become part of this president's platform, and what's significantly sad about it is, he just doesn't care. Since assuming office during 2016, President Trump has made 10,111 false or misleading statements according to Fact Checker. The numbers are growing by the day.

8. He is still refusing to turn over his taxes. If you have nothing to hide, why not follow the lead of others who came before you, Mr. President? Are you afraid that there will be money laundering, deals with Russia and Saudi Arabia, misquotes on your net worth, bankruptcy history, reneges

on debts? Just what is it? If you were totally exonerated by the Mueller report, then where is the transparency so that the American people can see your innocence or not?

9. The country is sinking under the weight of a divided government. Hate and bigotry are alive and well, and this president is a good example of what a bad leader can do to good organizations.

10. This president is more versed on the golf game than he is on running the country. He has little patience and desire to study international or domestic law. He reads too little and tweets too much.

11. The Republican Party is in shambles because the Senate, for which they have the majority, doesn't have the backbone to corral a rogue president who is riding roughshod over the most powerful country in the world on a bicycle with training wheels. He feels that he has nothing to lose if he doesn't get reelected in 2020 because he never wanted the job in the first place. His run for the presidency was no more than an ego trip and a promotion for his TV show. Meanwhile, as we suffer under the weight of his incompetence, he is destroying the fabric of a nation with a sharp tongue and weak mind.

REFERENCES

Blackburn, Robin. *The Overthrow of Colonial Slavery, 1776–1848*. New York: Verso Books, 1988. ISBN 0-86091-901-3.

Schwartz, Jon. "Colin Kaepernick Is Righter than You Know: The National Anthem Is a Celebration of Slavery." *The Intercept* (August 28, 2016). Read more at http://www.brainy quotes.com/quotes?src=t at: implicit.

Keehn, David. "3 Elements Needed for an Effective Mentorship Program." March 16, 2016.

Lomax, L. E. *When the Word Is Given*. 1964, repr. 1979.

Wales, Jimmy and Larry Sanger. Wikipedia, the Free Encyclopedia.

Kimberly Amadeo in November of 2018, and Elena Holodny and Andy Kiersz in December of 2017

www.ingramcontent.com/pod-product-compliance
Lightning Source LLC
Chambersburg PA
CBHW030240030426
42336CB00009B/187